Contents

Chef John's Pumpkin Pancakes 7

Roasted Acorn Squash Salad 8

Short Ribs Braised with Mushrooms and Tomatoes 9

Persimmon Bread II 10

Roasted Brussels Sprouts 11

Persimmon Bread II 12

Short Ribs Braised with Mushrooms and Tomatoes 13

Roasted Brussels Sprouts 14

Roasted Beets 'n' Sweets 15

Apple Crisp II 15

Brasato al Barolo - Braised Chuck Roast in Red Wine 16

Eggplant Parmesan II 18

Wedding Gift Spaghetti Sauce 18

Eggplant Mixed Grill 19

Spicy Zucchini Oatmeal Cookies 20

Pumpkin Gingerbread 21

Beef Stew VI 22

Chef John's Chicken and Dumplings 23

Autumn Cheesecake 24

Cranberry Upside-Down Sour Cream Cake 25

Three Bean Salad 26

Watergate Salad 27

Olive Oil Roasted Eggplant with Lemon 27

Pumpkin Spice Cupcakes 28

Classic Meatloaf 29

Best Ever Banana Bread 31

Downeast Maine Pumpkin Bread 32

Easy Fried Eggplant 33

Corn Fritters 33

Apple Turnovers 34

Cedar Planked Salmon 35

Butternut Squash Soup II 36

Beet Salad with Goat Cheese 37

Canned Apple Pie Filling 37

Pumpkin Spice 38

Cheese Fondue 39

Peach Preserves 39

Banana-Zucchini Bread 40

Apple Pie Filling 41

Country Style Green Beans with Red Potatoes 42

Fondant Potatoes 42

Quick Yeast Rolls 44

Grilled Pork Loin Chops 44

Two Ingredient Pumpkin Cake 45

Baked Oatmeal II 46

Apple Pie I 47

Napa Cabbage Salad 47

Pecan Pie Bars I 48

Acorn Squash 49

Homemade Apple Cider 50

Aunt Mary's Eggplant Balls 51

Ranch Oyster Crackers 51

Pumpkin Chocolate Chip Cookies III 52

Roquefort Pear Salad 53

Greek Lentil Soup (Fakes) 54

Gramma's Apple Bread Pudding 55

Chocolate Wave Zucchini Bread 56

No Sugar Apple Pie 57

Easy Apple Crisp 58

Apple Butter Spice Cake 58

German Apple Pancake 60

Roasted Duck 61

Roasted Roma Tomatoes 61

Chef John's Easy Apple Pie 62

Asian Marinated Pork Chops 63

Mexican Pumpkin Empanadas 64

Instant Pot Chicken and Dumplings 65

Pumpkin Roll I 67

Eggplant Parmesan I 68

Rachel's Cranberry Chicken Salad 69

Cranberry Pistachio Biscotti 69

Easy Pumpkin Muffins 70

Chef John's Pumpkin Pie 71

Autumn Rainbow Sheet Pan Dinner 72

Nana's Apple Crisp 73

Eggplant Croquettes 74

Apple Cake I 75

Pumpkin Spice Coffee Syrup 75

Apple Crisp III 76

Applesauce 77

Dutch Apple Pie with Oatmeal Streusel 77

Top Sirloin Roast 79

Pumpkin Crunch Cake 80

Caramel Apple Pork Chops 81

Apple Cake IV 82

Better Baked Beans 83

Pumpkin Spice Cookie 83

Chef John's Beef Goulash 84

Vegetarian Moussaka 85

Pure Maple Candy 87

Cosmo-Style Pomegranate Martini 87

Apple Pie in a Jar Drink 88

Classic Cherries Jubilee 88

Hot Crab Dip 89

White Chocolate and Cranberry Cookies 90

Apple Pie Spice Mix 91

Candied Apples II 91

Millionaire Pie 92

Pear or Apple Cobbler 92

Easy Apple Coffee Cake 93

Apple Crisp IV 94

Squash Relish 95

Aunt Carol's Apple Pie 96

Vegetarian Gravy 97

Pumpkin Pie Squares 98

Quick Apple Pie Bread 99

Mom's Applesauce Pancakes 100

Autumn Spiced Butternut Squash Bread 100

Apple Dumplings I 101

Apple Honey Bundt Cake 102

Chef John's Shepherd's Pie 103

Chocolate Chip Pumpkin Bread 104

Easy Chicken Marsala 105

Easiest Eggplant 106

Fresh Apple Walnut Cake 106

Holiday Chicken Salad 107

Easy Canned Venison 108

Easy Pumpkin Pie Squares 109

Apple Slab Pie 109

Apple Slab Pie 111

Pumpkin Dump Cake 112

Lime Gelatin Salad I 112

Bread and Celery Stuffing 113

Gorgonzola Cream Sauce 114

Creamy Mushroom Meatloaf 115

Ranch, Bacon, and Parmesan Pasta Salad 116

Pumpkin Pie Spice I 117

Roasted Garlic Parmesan Mashed Potatoes 118

Apple Scones 118

Easy Apple Rhubarb Jam 119

Grandma's Fresh Apple Cake 120

Apple and Tomato Chutney 121

Simple Swiss Chard 122

Apple Stuffed Pork Chops... 122

Country Banana Bread 123

Danish Pastry Apple Bars 124

Absolute Stress 125

Sheet Pan Roasted Vegetables... 125

Feta Cheese Foldovers 126

Applesauce Doughnuts 127

Savory Roasted Root Vegetables... 128

Best Ever Caramel Apple Crisp... 129

Chef John's Roasted Brussels Sprouts 130

Cheese and Sausage Stuffed Zucchini 130

Pumpkin Gingerbread 131

Dutch Apple Pie... 132

Bulk Venison Breakfast Sausage... 133

Arugula-Fennel Salad 134

Cheesy Meatloaf... 135

Steak N Gravy 135

Blushing Applesauce 136

Super Duper Easy Apple Cake 137

Grilled Eggplant Moussaka.. 137

Apple Butter Pork Loin.. 139

Best Zucchini Casserole 140

Dutch Apple Cake... 140

Chicken Savoy.. 141

Awesome Eggplant Rollatine 142

Pumpkin Dessert... 143

Pumpkin Cookies with Cream Cheese Frosting (The World's Best!) 144

Quick Brussels and Bacon.. 145

Banana Cranberry Bread 146

Squash and Zucchini Casserole 147

Sweet Potato Pie II 148

Apple Breakfast Bread 149

Easy Swedish Apple Pie 149

Zucchini with Chickpea and Mushroom Stuffing 150

Mexican Zucchini Cheese Soup 151

Chef John's Pumpkin Pancakes

Prep: 15 mins **Cook:** 45 mins **Total:** 1 hr **Servings:** 6 **Yield:** 6 servings

Ingredients

- 2 cups all-purpose flour
- 2 tablespoons brown sugar
- 1 tablespoon white sugar
- 2 teaspoons baking powder
- 1 teaspoon baking soda
- ½ teaspoon salt
- 1 cup pumpkin puree
- 1 teaspoon ground cinnamon
- ½ teaspoon ground ginger
- ½ teaspoon ground allspice
- 1 egg
- 1 ½ cups milk
- 2 tablespoons vegetable oil
- 2 tablespoons lemon juice
- 2 teaspoons grated lemon zest
- 1 teaspoon vegetable oil

Directions

Step 1

Combine flour, brown sugar, white sugar, baking powder, baking soda, and salt in a large mixing bowl, and whisk together for two minutes to aerate.

Step 2

In a separate bowl, combine pumpkin puree, cinnamon, ginger, allspice, egg, milk, 2 tablespoons of vegetable oil, lemon juice, and lemon zest. Mix in the flour mixture, and stir just until moistened. (Do not overmix.)

Step 3

Coat skillet with 1 teaspoon vegetable oil over medium heat.

Step 4

Pour batter into skillet 1/4 cup at a time, and cook the pancakes until golden brown, about 3 minutes on each side.

Nutrition Facts

Per Serving:

284.3 calories; protein 7.9g 16% DV; carbohydrates 46g 15% DV; fat 7.9g 12% DV; cholesterol 35.9mg 12% DV; sodium 703.6mg 28% DV.

Roasted Acorn Squash Salad

Prep: 30 mins **Cook:** 15 mins **Additional:** 30 mins **Total:** 1 hr 15 mins **Servings:** 4 **Yield:** 4 servings

Ingredients

- 1 acorn squash - peeled, seeded, and cut into 1-inch cubes
- 2 tablespoons olive oil
- ½ teaspoon ground cinnamon
- ½ teaspoon onion powder
- ½ teaspoon ground cumin
- ½ teaspoon salt
- ¼ teaspoon ground black pepper
- 3 tablespoons apple cider vinegar
- 2 tablespoons maple syrup
- 1 tablespoon Dijon mustard
- 1 teaspoon grated orange zest
- 1 teaspoon garam masala
- 1 clove garlic, minced
- ½ teaspoon salt
- ½ teaspoon ground black pepper
- ½ cup olive oil
- 1 (5 ounce) package baby arugula
- ¼ cup dried cranberries
- ¼ cup chopped pistachios
- 2 ounces crumbled chevre (goat cheese)

Directions

Step 1

Position a rack into the center position of the oven and preheat oven to 400 degrees F (200 degrees C). Line a baking sheet or jelly roll pan with parchment paper.

Step 2

Spread acorn squash cubes onto prepared baking sheet and toss with 2 tablespoons olive oil. Mix cinnamon, onion powder, cumin, 1/2 teaspoon salt, and 1/4 teaspoon black pepper in a small bowl; sprinkle spice mixture over squash cubes.

Step 3

Bake on the center rack of preheated oven until squash are tender, 15 to 20 minutes. Remove from oven and allow to cool completely.

Step 4

Whisk apple cider vinegar, maple syrup, Dijon mustard, orange zest, garam masala, garlic, 1/2 teaspoon salt, and 1/2 teaspoon black pepper in a bowl until thoroughly combined; slowly drizzle olive oil into vinegar mixture, whisking constantly, until olive oil incorporates into the dressing. Refrigerate while completing remaining steps.

Step 5

Toss cooked acorn squash cubes, baby arugula, cranberries, pistachios, and goat cheese in a salad bowl; drizzle with dressing and serve.

Cook's Note:

You can make the acorn squash and dressing the night before and store in your fridge to cut down on time also.

Nutrition Facts

Per Serving:

515.9 calories; protein 6.9g 14% DV; carbohydrates 32.1g 10% DV; fat 42.2g 65% DV; cholesterol 11.2mg 4% DV; sodium 798.1mg 32% DV.

Short Ribs Braised with Mushrooms and Tomatoes

Prep: 15 mins **Cook:** 2 hrs 15 mins **Additional:** 30 mins **Total:** 3 hrs **Servings:** 8 **Yield:** 8 servings

Ingredients

- ½ cup dried porcini mushrooms
- ½ cup water
- 2 ½ pounds beef short ribs
- 1 pinch salt and freshly ground black pepper to taste
- 2 tablespoons vegetable oil
- 1 onion, sliced
- 2 cloves garlic, minced
- 2 cups beef broth
- 1 cup tomato sauce
- 1 teaspoon dried rosemary
- ½ teaspoon salt
- 1 pinch cayenne pepper
- 1 bay leaf

Directions

Step 1

Combine mushrooms and water in a bowl; soak until mushrooms are rehydrated, about 30 minutes. Drain mushrooms and reserve liquid; dice mushrooms.

Step 2

Preheat oven to 325 degrees F (165 degrees C).

Step 3

Season short ribs all over with salt and black pepper.

Step 4

Heat vegetable oil in a skillet over medium-high heat. Cook short ribs in hot oil until browned on all sides, to 12 minutes. Transfer ribs to a Dutch oven.

Step 5

Return skillet to heat and saute onion with a pinch of salt in hot pan until softened, about 3 minutes. Add garlic and saute until fragrant, about 1 minute more. Stir mushrooms into onion mixture.

Step 6

Pour reserved mushroom liquid into skillet and bring to a boil while scraping the browned bits of food off of the bottom of the pan with a wooden spoon. Stir beef broth, tomato sauce, rosemary, 1/2 teaspoon salt, cayenne pepper, and bay leaf into onion mixture.

Step 7

Pour tomato mixture over short ribs into Dutch oven and cover Dutch oven with a lid.

Step 8

Cook short ribs in the preheated oven until short ribs are fork-tender, about 2 hours.

Nutrition Facts
Per Serving:
362.4 calories; protein 16.5g 33% DV; carbohydrates 6.3g 2% DV; fat 29.9g 46% DV; cholesterol 58.3mg 19% DV; sodium 556.9mg 22% DV.

Persimmon Bread II

Prep: 10 mins **Cook:** 1 hr **Total:** 1 hr 10 mins **Servings:** 24 **Yield:** 3 - 6x3 inch loaves

Ingredients

- 1 cup persimmon pulp
- 2 teaspoons baking soda
- 3 cups white sugar
- 1 cup vegetable oil
- 4 large eggs eggs
- 1 ½ teaspoons ground cinnamon

- ½ teaspoon ground nutmeg
- 1 ½ teaspoons salt
- ⅔ cup water
- 3 cups all-purpose flour
- 1 cup chopped walnuts

Directions

Step 1

Preheat the oven to 350 degrees F (175 degrees C). Grease three 6x3 inch loaf pans.

Step 2

In a small bowl, stir together the persimmon pulp and baking soda. Let stand 5 minutes to thicken the pulp.

Step 3

In a medium bowl, combine sugar, oil, eggs, cinnamon, nutmeg, and salt. Blend until smooth. Mix in persimmon pulp and water alternately with flour. Fold in nuts. Divide batter into the prepared pans, filling each pan 2/3 full.

Step 4

Bake for 1 hour in the preheated oven, or until a toothpick inserted comes out clean. Cool in pan for 10 minutes before removing to a wire rack to cool completely.

Nutrition Facts

Per Serving:

291.6 calories; protein 3.5g 7% DV; carbohydrates 41.1g 13% DV; fat 13.4g 21% DV; cholesterol 31mg 10% DV; sodium 262.4mg 11% DV.

Roasted Brussels Sprouts

Prep: 15 mins **Cook:** 45 mins **Total:** 1 hr **Servings:** 6 **Yield:** 6 servings

Ingredients

- 1 ½ pounds Brussels sprouts, ends trimmed and yellow leaves removed
- 3 tablespoons olive oil
- 1 teaspoon kosher salt
- ½ teaspoon freshly ground black pepper

Directions

Step 1

Preheat oven to 400 degrees F (205 degrees C).

Step 2

Place trimmed Brussels sprouts, olive oil, kosher salt, and pepper in a large resealable plastic bag. Seal tightly, and shake to coat. Pour onto a baking sheet, and place on center oven rack.

Step 3

Roast in the preheated oven for 30 to 45 minutes, shaking pan every 5 to 7 minutes for even browning. Reduce heat when necessary to prevent burning. Brussels sprouts should be darkest brown, almost black, when done. Adjust seasoning with kosher salt, if necessary. Serve immediately.

Nutrition Facts

Per Serving:

104.4 calories; protein 2.9g 6% DV; carbohydrates 10g 3% DV; fat 7.3g 11% DV; cholesterolmg; sodium 344mg 14% DV.

Persimmon Bread II

Prep: 10 mins **Cook:** 1 hr **Total:** 1 hr 10 mins **Servings:** 24 **Yield:** 3 - 6x3 inch loaves

Ingredients

- 1 cup persimmon pulp
- 2 teaspoons baking soda
- 3 cups white sugar
- 1 cup vegetable oil
- 4 large eggs eggs
- 1 ½ teaspoons ground cinnamon
- ½ teaspoon ground nutmeg
- 1 ½ teaspoons salt
- ⅔ cup water
- 3 cups all-purpose flour
- 1 cup chopped walnuts

Directions

Step 1

Preheat the oven to 350 degrees F (175 degrees C). Grease three 6x3 inch loaf pans.

Step 2

In a small bowl, stir together the persimmon pulp and baking soda. Let stand 5 minutes to thicken the pulp.

Step 3

In a medium bowl, combine sugar, oil, eggs, cinnamon, nutmeg, and salt. Blend until smooth. Mix in persimmon pulp and water alternately with flour. Fold in nuts. Divide batter into the prepared pans, filling each pan 2/3 full.

Step 4

Bake for 1 hour in the preheated oven, or until a toothpick inserted comes out clean. Cool in pan for 10 minutes before removing to a wire rack to cool completely.

Short Ribs Braised with Mushrooms and Tomatoes

Prep: 15 mins **Cook:** 2 hrs 15 mins **Additional:** 30 mins **Total:** 3 hrs **Servings:** 8 **Yield:** 8 servings

Ingredients

- ½ cup dried porcini mushrooms
- ½ cup water
- 2 ½ pounds beef short ribs
- 1 pinch salt and freshly ground black pepper to taste
- 2 tablespoons vegetable oil
- 1 onion, sliced
- 2 cloves garlic, minced
- 2 cups beef broth
- 1 cup tomato sauce
- 1 teaspoon dried rosemary
- ½ teaspoon salt
- 1 pinch cayenne pepper
- 1 bay leaf

Directions

Step 1

Combine mushrooms and water in a bowl; soak until mushrooms are rehydrated, about 30 minutes. Drain mushrooms and reserve liquid; dice mushrooms.

Step 2

Preheat oven to 325 degrees F (165 degrees C).

Step 3

Season short ribs all over with salt and black pepper.

Step 4

Heat vegetable oil in a skillet over medium-high heat. Cook short ribs in hot oil until browned on all sides, 7 to 12 minutes. Transfer ribs to a Dutch oven.

Step 5

Return skillet to heat and saute onion with a pinch of salt in hot pan until softened, about 3 minutes. Add garlic and saute until fragrant, about 1 minute more. Stir mushrooms into onion mixture.

Step 6

Pour reserved mushroom liquid into skillet and bring to a boil while scraping the browned bits of food off o the bottom of the pan with a wooden spoon. Stir beef broth, tomato sauce, rosemary, 1/2 teaspoon salt, cayenne pepper, and bay leaf into onion mixture.

Step 7

Pour tomato mixture over short ribs into Dutch oven and cover Dutch oven with a lid.

Step 8

Cook short ribs in the preheated oven until short ribs are fork-tender, about 2 hours.

Nutrition Facts
Per Serving:
362.4 calories; protein 16.5g 33% DV; carbohydrates 6.3g 2% DV; fat 29.9g 46% DV; cholesterol 58.3mg 19% DV; sodium 556.9mg 22% DV.

Roasted Brussels Sprouts

Prep: 15 mins **Cook:** 45 mins **Total:** 1 hr **Servings:** 6 **Yield:** 6 servings

Ingredients

- 1 ½ pounds Brussels sprouts, ends trimmed and yellow leaves removed
- 3 tablespoons olive oil
- 1 teaspoon kosher salt
- ½ teaspoon freshly ground black pepper

Directions

Step 1

Preheat oven to 400 degrees F (205 degrees C).

Step 2

Place trimmed Brussels sprouts, olive oil, kosher salt, and pepper in a large resealable plastic bag. Seal tightly, and shake to coat. Pour onto a baking sheet, and place on center oven rack.

Step 3

Roast in the preheated oven for 30 to 45 minutes, shaking pan every 5 to 7 minutes for even browning. Reduce heat when necessary to prevent burning. Brussels sprouts should be darkest brown, almost black, when done. Adjust seasoning with kosher salt, if necessary. Serve immediately.

Nutrition Facts

Per Serving:

104.4 calories; protein 2.9g 6% DV; carbohydrates 10g 3% DV; fat 7.3g 11% DV; cholesterolmg; sodium 344mg 14% DV.

Roasted Beets 'n' Sweets

Prep: 15 mins **Cook:** 1 hr **Total:** 1 hr 15 mins **Servings:** 6 **Yield:** 6 servings

Ingredients

- 6 medium beets, peeled and cut into chunks
- 2 ½ tablespoons olive oil, divided
- 1 teaspoon garlic powder
- 1 teaspoon kosher salt
- 1 teaspoon ground black pepper
- 1 teaspoon sugar
- 3 medium sweet potatoes, cut into chunks
- 1 large sweet onion, chopped

Directions

Step 1

Preheat oven to 400 degrees F (200 degrees C).

Step 2

In a bowl, toss the beets with 1/2 tablespoon olive oil to coat. Spread in a single layer on a baking sheet.

Step 3

Mix the remaining 2 tablespoons olive oil, garlic powder, salt, pepper, and sugar in a large resealable plastic bag. Place the sweet potatoes and onion in the bag. Seal bag, and shake to coat vegetables with the oil mixture.

Step 4

Bake beets 15 minutes in the preheated oven. Mix sweet potato mixture with the beets on the baking sheet. Continue baking 45 minutes, stirring after 20 minutes, until all vegetables are tender.

Nutrition Facts

Per Serving:

195 calories; protein 3.5g 7% DV; carbohydrates 33.6g 11% DV; fat 5.9g 9% DV; cholesterolmg; sodium 447.8mg 18% DV.

Apple Crisp II

Prep: 30 mins **Cook:** 45 mins **Additional:** 5 mins **Total:** 1 hr 20 mins **Servings:** 12 **Yield:** 1 9x13-inch pan

Ingredients

- 10 cups all-purpose apples, peeled, cored and sliced
- 1 cup white sugar
- 1 tablespoon all-purpose flour

- 1 teaspoon ground cinnamon
- ½ cup water
- 1 cup quick-cooking oats
- 1 cup all-purpose flour
- 1 cup packed brown sugar
- ¼ teaspoon baking powder
- ¼ teaspoon baking soda
- ½ cup butter, melted

Directions

Step 1

Preheat oven to 350 degrees F (175 degree C).

Step 2

Place the sliced apples in a 9x13 inch pan. Mix the white sugar, 1 tablespoon flour and ground cinnamon together, and sprinkle over apples. Pour water evenly over all.

Step 3

Combine the oats, 1 cup flour, brown sugar, baking powder, baking soda and melted butter together. Crumble evenly over the apple mixture.

Step 4

Bake at 350 degrees F (175 degrees C) for about 45 minutes.

Nutrition Facts

Per Serving:

316 calories; protein 2.4g 5% DV; carbohydrates 60.5g 20% DV; fat 8.4g 13% DV; cholesterol 20.3mg 7% DV; sodium 97.9mg 4% DV.

Brasato al Barolo - Braised Chuck Roast in Red Wine

Prep: 30 mins **Cook:** 2 hrs 46 mins **Additional:** 12 hrs **Total:** 15 hrs 16 mins **Servings:** 5 **Yield:** 1 2-pound roast

Ingredients

- 1 (2 pound) beef chuck roast
- 1 onion, cut into 8 pieces, layers separated
- 2 large carrots, cut into 1-inch pieces
- 2 ribs celery, cut into 1-inch pieces
- 10 eaches whole black peppercorns
- 5 eaches whole cloves

- 1 clove garlic, crushed
- 1 cinnamon stick
- 1 sprig rosemary
- 2 leaf (blank)s bay leaves
- 1 (750 milliliter) bottle Barolo (dry Italian) red wine
- 3 tablespoons olive oil, or more to taste
- 1 teaspoon salt

Directions

Step 1

Place chuck roast, onion, carrots, celery, peppercorns, cloves, garlic, cinnamon stick, rosemary, and bay leaves together in a stockpot. Pour wine over meat and vegetable mixture to cover entirely. Cover stockpot and marinate for 6 hours in the refrigerator. Turn meat in marinade to make sure it is completely covered; return to refrigerator to finish marinating, about 6 hours more.

Step 2

Transfer chuck roast from marinade to a plate to rest; pat dry thoroughly with paper towels. Pour marinade through a strainer and into a bowl to separate vegetable mixture from wine, reserving both vegetable mixture and wine.

Step 3

Heat olive oil in the stockpot over medium-high heat. Brown chuck roast on all sides, 4 to 6 minutes per side. Reduce heat to medium. Add strained vegetable mixture to stockpot; cook with the chuck roast until fragrant, adding more oil as necessary to prevent burning, about 8 minutes.

Step 4

Pour reserved wine back into stockpot; add salt. Reduce heat to medium-low, cover, and simmer without removing cover for 2 hours. Remove cover, stir, and cook until meat easily shreds with a fork, 10 minutes to 1 hour longer. Transfer meat from cooking liquid to serving platter; tent with foil to keep warm.

Step 5

Return cooking liquid to a boil over medium-high heat; simmer until reduced to sauce consistency, 20 to 30 minutes. Discard cinnamon stick, rosemary, and bay leaves. Season with salt; puree mixture with a handheld immersion blender until smooth. Pour sauce over meat to serve.

Cook's Note:

If you can't find Barolo wine, use a hearty dry red wine.

Nutrition Facts

Per Serving:

517.2 calories; protein 22.5g 45% DV; carbohydrates 14.1g 5% DV; fat 28.8g 44% DV; cholesterol 82.6mg 28% DV; sodium 568mg 23% DV.

Eggplant Parmesan II

Prep: 25 mins **Cook:** 35 mins **Total:** 1 hr **Servings:** 10 **Yield:** 8 to 10 servings

Ingredients

- 3 eggplant, peeled (yield from 1.25 lb)s eggplant, peeled and thinly sliced
- 2 large eggs eggs, beaten
- 4 cups Italian seasoned bread crumbs
- 6 cups spaghetti sauce, divided
- 1 (16 ounce) package mozzarella cheese, shredded and divided
- ½ cup grated Parmesan cheese, divided
- ½ teaspoon dried basil

Directions

Step 1

Preheat oven to 350 degrees F (175 degrees C).

Step 2

Dip eggplant slices in egg, then in bread crumbs. Place in a single layer on a baking sheet. Bake in preheated oven for 5 minutes on each side.

Step 3

In a 9x13 inch baking dish spread spaghetti sauce to cover the bottom. Place a layer of eggplant slices in the sauce. Sprinkle with mozzarella and Parmesan cheeses. Repeat with remaining ingredients, ending with the cheeses. Sprinkle basil on top.

Step 4

Bake in preheated oven for 35 minutes, or until golden brown.

Nutrition Facts

Per Serving:

487.4 calories; protein 24.2g 48% DV; carbohydrates 62.1g 20% DV; fat 16g 25% DV; cholesterol 72.8mg 24% DV; sodium 1663.1mg 67% DV.

Wedding Gift Spaghetti Sauce

Prep: 10 mins **Cook:** 2 hrs 30 mins **Total:** 2 hrs 40 mins **Servings:** 30 **Yield:** 30 servings

Ingredients

- ½ cup butter
- 3 tablespoons olive oil
- 1 large onion, chopped
- 3 cloves garlic, chopped

- 1 pound ground beef
- 1 pound mild sausage
- 4 teaspoons Italian seasoning
- 2 teaspoons salt
- 2 teaspoons dried rosemary
- 1 ½ teaspoons dried oregano
- ½ teaspoon ground black pepper
- 76 fluid ounces water
- 1 (29 ounce) can tomato puree
- 3 (6 ounce) cans tomato paste

Directions

Step 1

Heat butter and olive oil together with onion and garlic in a large pot over medium heat; cook and stir ground beef and sausage in the onion mixture until browned and crumbly, 10 to 15 minutes. Stir Italian seasoning, salt, rosemary, oregano, and black pepper into ground beef-sausage mixture; simmer for 20 minutes.

Step 2

Pour water, tomato puree, and tomato paste into ground beef-sausage mixture; simmer, stirring occasionally, over low heat until flavors have combined, at least 2 hours.

Nutrition Facts

Per Serving:

137.2 calories; protein 5.9g 12% DV; carbohydrates 6.5g 2% DV; fat 10.2g 16% DV; cholesterol 26.1mg 9% DV; sodium 564mg 23% DV.

Eggplant Mixed Grill

Prep: 15 mins **Cook:** 12 mins **Additional:** 2 hrs 3 mins **Total:** 2 hrs 30 mins **Servings:** 6 **Yield:** 6 servings

Ingredients

- 2 tablespoons olive oil
- 2 tablespoons chopped fresh parsley
- 2 tablespoons chopped fresh oregano
- 2 tablespoons chopped fresh basil
- 1 tablespoon balsamic vinegar
- 1 teaspoon kosher salt
- ½ teaspoon black pepper
- 6 cloves garlic, minced
- 1 red onion, cut into wedges

- 18 spears fresh asparagus, trimmed
- 12 medium (blank)s crimini mushrooms, stems removed
- 1 (1 pound) eggplant, sliced into 1/4 inch rounds
- 1 red bell pepper, cut into wedges
- 1 yellow bell pepper, cut into wedges

Directions

Step 1

In a large resealable plastic bag, mix the olive oil, parsley, oregano, basil, vinegar, kosher salt, pepper, and garlic. Place the onion, asparagus, mushrooms, eggplant, red bell pepper, and yellow bell pepper into the bag. Seal, and marinate 2 hours in the refrigerator, turning occasionally

Step 2

Preheat the grill for high heat.

Step 3

- Lightly oil the grill grate. Grill the vegetables 6 minutes on each side, until tender.

Nutrition Facts

Per Serving:

106.8 calories; protein 4.3g 9% DV; carbohydrates 13.3g 4% DV; fat 4.9g 8% DV; cholesterolmg; sodium 340.4mg 14% DV.

Spicy Zucchini Oatmeal Cookies

Prep: 15 mins **Cook:** 15 mins **Total:** 30 mins **Servings:** 30 **Yield:** 2 1/2 dozen cookies

Ingredients

- 1 ¼ cups all-purpose flour
- ½ teaspoon baking soda
- 1 ½ teaspoons ground cinnamon
- ¼ teaspoon ground cloves
- ½ cup butter, softened
- ⅔ cup packed brown sugar
- 1 egg
- 1 teaspoon vanilla extract
- 1 cup quick cooking oats
- 1 cup shredded zucchini
- ½ cup raisins

Directions

Step 1

Preheat an oven to 350 degrees F (175 degrees C). Grease baking sheets.

Step 2

Stir together the flour, baking soda, cinnamon, and cloves in a bowl; set aside. Beat the butter and brown sugar with an electric mixer in a large bowl until creamy. Add the egg and the vanilla extract. Mix in the flour mixture and oats until just incorporated.

Step 3

Wring the zucchini in a clean towel to remove any excess moisture. Stir the zucchini and raisins into the dough; mixing just enough to evenly combine. Drop batter by rounded teaspoonfuls 2-inches apart onto the prepared baking sheets. Bake for 14 to 16 minutes or until the bottom edges turn golden brown.

Nutrition Facts

Per Serving:

85.9 calories; protein 1.3g 3% DV; carbohydrates 12.8g 4% DV; fat 3.5g 5% DV; cholesterol 14.3mg 5% DV; sodium 47.5mg 2% DV.

Pumpkin Gingerbread

Prep: 15 mins **Cook:** 45 mins **Total:** 1 hr **Servings:** 24 **Yield:** 2 - 9x5 inch loaves

Ingredients

- 3 cups sugar
- 1 cup vegetable oil
- 4 large eggs eggs
- ⅔ cup water
- 1 (15 ounce) can pumpkin puree
- 2 teaspoons ground ginger
- 1 teaspoon ground allspice
- 1 teaspoon ground cinnamon
- 1 teaspoon ground cloves
- 3 ½ cups all-purpose flour
- 2 teaspoons baking soda
- 1 ½ teaspoons salt
- ½ teaspoon baking powder

Directions

Step 1

Preheat oven to 350 degrees F (175 degrees C). Lightly grease two 9x5 inch loaf pans.

Step 2

In a large mixing, combine sugar, oil and eggs; beat until smooth. Add water and beat until well blended. Stir in pumpkin, ginger, allspice cinnamon, and clove.

Step 3

In medium bowl, combine flour, soda, salt, and baking powder. Add dry ingredients to pumpkin mixture and blend just until all ingredients are mixed. Divide batter between prepared pans.

Step 4

Bake in preheated oven until toothpick comes out clean, about 1 hour.

Nutrition Facts

Per Serving:

262.6 calories; protein 3.2g 6% DV; carbohydrates 40.7g 13% DV; fat 10.2g 16% DV; cholesterol 31mg 10% DV; sodium 313.1mg 13% DV.

Beef Stew VI

Prep: 20 mins **Cook:** 2 hrs **Total:** 2 hrs 20 mins **Servings:** 10 **Yield:** 10 servings

Ingredients

- 2 pounds cubed beef stew meat
- 3 tablespoons vegetable oil
- 4 cubes beef bouillon, crumbled
- 4 cups water
- 1 teaspoon dried rosemary
- 1 teaspoon dried parsley
- ½ teaspoon ground black pepper
- 3 large potatoes, peeled and cubed
- 4 medium (blank)s carrots, cut into 1 inch pieces
- 4 stalks celery, cut into 1 inch pieces
- 1 large onion, chopped
- 2 teaspoons cornstarch
- 2 teaspoons cold water

Directions

Step 1

In a large pot or dutch oven, cook beef in oil over medium heat until brown. Dissolve bouillon in water and pour into pot. Stir in rosemary, parsley and pepper. Bring to a boil, then reduce heat, cover and simmer 1 hour.

Step 2

Stir potatoes, carrots, celery, and onion into the pot. Dissolve cornstarch in 2 teaspoons cold water and stir into stew. Cover and simmer 1 hour more.

Nutrition Facts

Per Serving:

401.1 calories; protein 27.2g 54% DV; carbohydrates 24.9g 8% DV; fat 21.2g 33% DV; cholesterol 79mg 26% DV; sodium 436.3mg 18% DV.

Chef John's Chicken and Dumplings

Prep: 15 mins **Cook:** 1 hr 45 mins **Total:** 2 hrs **Servings:** 4 **Yield:** 4 servings

Ingredients

- 1 (3 to 3 1/2 pound) whole chicken
- 2 ½ quarts cold water
- 1 large carrot, cubed
- 1 stalk celery, chopped
- 1 onion, chopped
- 3 sprigs fresh thyme
- 1 bay leaf
- 2 tablespoons all-purpose flour, or as needed
- 1 pinch salt and freshly ground black pepper to taste
- ½ teaspoon cayenne pepper, or more to taste
- ½ cup creme fraiche
- ½ cup milk
- 2 teaspoons chopped fresh thyme leaves
- 2 eaches eggs
- 2 cups self-rising flour
- 4 sprigs thyme, for garnish

Directions

Step 1

Place chicken in a Dutch oven. Add water, carrot, celery, onion, 3 sprigs of thyme, and bay leaf. Bring to a boil, cover, reduce heat to low, and simmer for 1 hour. Remove chicken from dutch oven and transfer to a bowl; set aside to cool.

Step 2

Increase heat and bring the stock to a simmer. Skim off any chicken fat that appears on top of the stock and reserve in a bowl. Combine 2 to 3 tablespoons of the reserved fat with flour in a small bowl; stir to make a paste, adding more flour if needed. Add the chicken fat and flour mixture to the stock. Reduce heat and simmer for 15 minutes.

Step 3

Remove chicken meat from the carcass and add to the stock. Season with salt, black pepper, and cayenne pepper to taste. Continue simmering for 10 to 15 minutes.

Step 4

Whisk creme fraiche, milk, 2 teaspoons of thyme leaves, and eggs together in a large bowl. Stir in self-rising flour until almost entirely incorporated; do not overmix.

Step 5

Scoop large dollops of dumpling mixture on top of the chicken stock. Increase heat slightly to medium-high. Cover and simmer until dumplings appear light and fluffy, and a toothpick inserted into the center comes out clean, 10 to 15 minutes. Serve garnish with thyme sprigs.

Chef's Note:

If you don't have self-rising flour (which does work better here) you can use 2 cups all-purpose flour sifted with 3 teaspoons baking powder and 1 teaspoon fine table salt.

Nutrition Facts

Per Serving:

750.3 calories; protein 43.7g 87% DV; carbohydrates 59.7g 19% DV; fat 36.8g 57% DV; cholesterol 217.2mg 72% DV; sodium 1011.9mg 41% DV.

Autumn Cheesecake

Prep: 30 mins **Cook:** 1 hr 10 mins **Additional:** 2 hrs 20 mins **Total:** 4 hrs **Servings:** 12 **Yield:** 1 - 9 inch springform

Ingredients

- 1 cup graham cracker crumbs
- ½ cup finely chopped pecans
- 3 tablespoons white sugar
- ½ teaspoon ground cinnamon
- ¼ cup unsalted butter, melted
- 2 (8 ounce) packages cream cheese, softened
- ½ cup white sugar
- 2 large eggs eggs
- ½ teaspoon vanilla extract
- 4 cups apples - peeled, cored and thinly sliced
- ⅓ cup white sugar
- ½ teaspoon ground cinnamon
- ¼ cup chopped pecans

Directions

Step 1

Preheat oven to 350 degrees F (175 degrees C). In a large bowl, stir together the graham cracker crumbs, 1/2 cup finely chopped pecans, 3 tablespoons sugar, 1/2 teaspoon cinnamon and melted butter; press into the bottom of a 9 inch springform pan. Bake in preheated oven for 10 minutes.

Step 2

In a large bowl, combine cream cheese and 1/2 cup sugar. Mix at medium speed until smooth. Beat in eggs one at a time, mixing well after each addition. Blend in vanilla; pour filling into the baked crust.

Step 3

In a small bowl, stir together 1/3 cup sugar and 1/2 teaspoon cinnamon. Toss the cinnamon-sugar with the apples to coat. Spoon apple mixture over cream cheese layer and sprinkle with 1/4 cup chopped pecans.

Step 4

Bake in preheated oven for 60 to 70 minutes. With a knife, loosen cake from rim of pan. Let cool, then remove the rim of pan. Chill cake before serving.

Nutrition Facts

Per Serving:

341.3 calories; protein 5.1g 10% DV; carbohydrates 30.3g 10% DV; fat 23.4g 36% DV; cholesterol 82.2mg 27% DV; sodium 165.5mg 7% DV.

Cranberry Upside-Down Sour Cream Cake

Prep: 20 mins **Cook:** 1 hr **Additional:** 10 mins **Total:** 1 hr 30 mins **Servings:** 12 **Yield:** 1 9-inch springform pan

Ingredients

- ½ cup butter
- 2 cups white sugar
- 2 tablespoons water
- 1 teaspoon ground cinnamon
- 1 (12 ounce) bag fresh or frozen cranberries
- 1 ½ cups cake flour
- ½ teaspoon baking soda
- ½ teaspoon salt
- 6 tablespoons butter, softened
- ½ cup white sugar
- ½ cup brown sugar
- 2 large eggs eggs
- 1 teaspoon vanilla extract

- ¾ cup sour cream

Directions

Step 1

Preheat the oven to 350 degrees F (175 degrees C). Generously grease a 9 inch springform pan. Wrap aluminum foil around the outside of the bottom to prevent leaking.

Step 2

Melt the butter in a saucepan over medium heat. Stir in 1 1/2 cups of white sugar, water and cinnamon until sugar has dissolved. Bring to a boil and then add the cranberries. Stir to coat with the sauce, then pour into the prepared pan.

Step 3

Sift together the flour, baking soda and salt; set aside. In a medium bowl, beat the remaining 6 tablespoons of butter with 1/2 cup white sugar and brown sugar until light and fluffy. Mix in the eggs one at a time, beating well after each addition. Stir in vanilla and sour cream. Mix in the dry ingredients. Pour the batter over the cranberries in the pan.

Step 4

Bake for about 50 minutes in the preheated oven, or until a knife inserted into the center comes out clean. Cool on a rack for 10 minutes, then run a knife around the outer edge. Invert onto a serving plate and remove the springform pan.

Nutrition Facts

Per Serving:

436.7 calories; protein 3.2g 7% DV; carbohydrates 68.9g 22% DV; fat 17.5g 27% DV; cholesterol 72.9mg 24% DV; sodium 267.6mg 11% DV.

Three Bean Salad

Servings: 16 **Yield:** 16 servings

Ingredients

- 1 (15 ounce) can green beans
- 1 pound wax beans
- 1 (15 ounce) can kidney beans, drained and rinsed
- 1 onion, sliced into thin rings
- ¾ cup white sugar
- ⅔ cup distilled white vinegar
- ⅓ cup vegetable oil
- ½ teaspoon salt
- ½ teaspoon ground black pepper
- ½ teaspoon celery seed

Directions

Step 1

Mix together green beans, wax beans, kidney beans, onion, sugar, vinegar, vegetable oil, salt, pepper, and celery seed. Let set in refrigerator for at least 12 hours.

Nutrition Facts

Per Serving:

111.5 calories; protein 2g 4% DV; carbohydrates 15.9g 5% DV; fat 4.7g 7% DV; cholesterolmg; sodium 298.6mg 12% DV.

Watergate Salad

Prep: 10 mins **Additional:** 2 hrs **Total:** 2 hrs 10 mins **Servings:** 8 **Yield:** 8 servings

Ingredients

- 1 (3.4 ounce) package instant pistachio pudding mix
- 1 (8 ounce) can crushed pineapple, with juice
- 1 cup miniature marshmallows
- ½ cup chopped walnuts
- ½ (8 ounce) container frozen whipped topping, thawed

Directions

Step 1

In a large bowl, mix together pudding mix, pineapple with juice, marshmallows, and nuts. Fold in whipped topping. Chill.

Nutrition Facts

Per Serving:

173.4 calories; protein 1.2g 3% DV; carbohydrates 24.6g 8% DV; fat 7.4g 11% DV; cholesterolmg; sodium 179.6mg 7% DV.

Olive Oil Roasted Eggplant with Lemon

Prep: 15 mins **Cook:** 25 mins **Total:** 40 mins **Servings:** 4 **Yield:** 4 servings

Ingredients

- 1 large eggplant
- 3 tablespoons extra virgin olive oil
- 1 pinch salt and pepper to taste
- 2 tablespoons fresh lemon juice

Directions

Step 1

Preheat the oven to 400 degrees F (200 degrees C). Line a baking sheet with parchment paper or lightly grease.

Step 2

Slice the eggplant in half lengthwise, then cut each half into quarters lengthwise. Cut each of those in half to make two shorter quarters. Place the eggplant onto the baking sheet with the skin side down. Brush each piece with olive oil and season with salt and pepper.

Step 3

Roast in the preheated oven until softened and golden brown, 25 to 30 minutes. Remove from the oven and sprinkle with lemon juice. Serve hot.

Nutrition Facts

Per Serving:

120.5 calories; protein 1.2g 2% DV; carbohydrates 7.2g 2% DV; fat 10.3g 16% DV; cholesterolmg; sodium 2.4mg.

Pumpkin Spice Cupcakes

Prep: 25 mins **Cook:** 25 mins **Additional:** 50 mins **Total:** 1 hr 40 mins **Servings:** 24 **Yield:** 24 cupcakes

Ingredients

- 2 ¼ cups all-purpose flour
- 1 teaspoon ground cinnamon
- ½ teaspoon ground nutmeg
- ½ teaspoon ground ginger
- ½ teaspoon ground cloves
- ½ teaspoon ground allspice
- ½ teaspoon salt
- 1 tablespoon baking powder
- ½ teaspoon baking soda
- ½ cup butter, softened
- 1 cup white sugar
- ⅓ cup brown sugar
- 2 large eggs eggs, room temperature
- ¾ cup milk
- 1 cup pumpkin puree
- Cinnamon Cream Cheese Frosting
- 1 (8 ounce) package cream cheese, softened
- ¼ cup butter, softened
- 3 cups confectioners' sugar

- 1 teaspoon vanilla extract
- 1 teaspoon ground cinnamon

Directions

Step 1

Preheat an oven to 375 degrees F (190 degrees C). Grease 24 muffin cups, or line with paper muffin liners. Sift together the flour, 1 teaspoon cinnamon, nutmeg, ginger, clove, allspice, salt, baking powder, and baking soda; set aside.

Step 2

Beat 1/2 cup of butter, the white sugar, and brown sugar with an electric mixer in a large bowl until light and fluffy. The mixture should be noticeably lighter in color. Add the room-temperature eggs one at a time, allowing each egg to blend into the butter mixture before adding the next. Stir in the milk and pumpkin puree after the last egg. Stir in the flour mixture, mixing until just incorporated. Pour the batter into the prepared muffin cups.

Step 3

Bake in the preheated oven until golden and the tops spring back when lightly pressed, about 25 minutes. Cool in the pans for 5 minutes before removing to cool completely on a wire rack.

Step 4

While the cupcakes are cooling, make the frosting by beating the cream cheese and 1/4 butter with an electric mixer in a bowl until smooth. Beat in the confectioners' sugar a little at a time until incorporated. Add the vanilla extract and 1 teaspoon ground cinnamon; beat until fluffy. Once the cupcakes are cool, frost with the cream cheese icing.

Nutrition Facts

Per Serving:

243.9 calories; protein 2.9g 6% DV; carbohydrates 37.2g 12% DV; fat 9.8g 15% DV; cholesterol 41.6mg 14% DV; sodium 220.1mg 9% DV.

Classic Meatloaf

Prep: 30 mins **Cook:** 45 mins **Total:** 1 hr 15 mins **Servings:** 10 **Yield:** 1 meatloaf

Ingredients

- 1 carrot, coarsely chopped
- 1 rib celery, coarsely chopped
- ½ onion, coarsely chopped
- ½ red bell pepper, coarsely chopped
- 4 medium (blank)s white mushrooms, coarsely chopped
- 3 cloves garlic, coarsely chopped
- 2 ½ pounds ground chuck

- 1 tablespoon Worcestershire sauce
- 1 egg, beaten
- 1 teaspoon dried Italian herbs
- 2 teaspoons salt
- 1 teaspoon ground black pepper
- ½ teaspoon cayenne pepper
- 1 cup plain bread crumbs
- 1 teaspoon olive oil

Glaze Ingredients:

- 2 tablespoons brown sugar
- 2 tablespoons ketchup
- 2 tablespoons Dijon mustard
- 1 dash hot pepper sauce to taste

Directions

Step 1

Preheat the oven to 325 degrees F.

Step 2

Place the carrot, celery, onion, red bell pepper, mushrooms, and garlic in a food processor, and pulse until very finely chopped, almost to a puree. Place the minced vegetables into a large mixing bowl, and mix in ground chuck, Worcestershire sauce, and egg. Add Italian herbs, salt, black pepper, and cayenne pepper. Mix gently with a wooden spoon to incorporate vegetables and egg into the meat. Pour in bread crumbs. With your hand, gently mix in the crumbs with your fingertips just until combined, about 1 minute.

Step 3

Form the meatloaf into a ball. Pour olive oil into a baking dish and place the ball of meat into the dish. Shape the ball into a loaf, about 4 inches high by 6 inches across.

Step 4

Bake in the preheated oven just until the meatloaf is hot, about 15 minutes.

Step 5

Meanwhile, in a small bowl, mix together brown sugar, ketchup, Dijon mustard, and hot sauce. Stir until the brown sugar has dissolved.

Step 6

Remove the meatloaf from the oven. With the back of a spoon, smooth the glaze onto the top of the meatloaf, then pull a little bit of glaze down the sides of the meatloaf with the back of the spoon.

Step 7

Return meatloaf to oven, and bake until the loaf is no longer pink inside and the glaze has baked onto the loaf, 30 to 40 more minutes. An instant-read thermometer inserted into the thickest part of the loaf should read at least 160 degrees F (70 degrees C). Cooking time will depend on shape and thickness of the meatloaf.

Cook's Note:

The shape, thickness, and type of baking pan you use will affect how long this meatloaf needs to be in the oven. Total time could take up to an hour or more. So be sure to check the internal temperature to ensure doneness.

Nutrition Facts
Per Serving:

284.1 calories; protein 21.6g 43% DV; carbohydrates 14.8g 5% DV; fat 14.9g 23% DV; cholesterol 85.3mg 28% DV; sodium 755.4mg 30% DV.

Best Ever Banana Bread

Servings: 12 **Yield:** 1 - 9x5 inch loaf

Ingredients

- 2 large eggs eggs, beaten
- ⅓ cup buttermilk
- ½ cup vegetable oil
- 1 cup mashed bananas
- 1 ½ cups white sugar
- 1 ¾ cups all-purpose flour
- 1 teaspoon baking soda
- ½ teaspoon salt
- ½ cup chopped pecans

Directions
Step 1

Preheat oven to 325 degrees F (165 degrees C). Spray one 9x5 inch loaf pan with non-stick spray coating.
Step 2

Blend together the eggs, buttermilk, oil and bananas.
Step 3

Sift together the sugar, flour, baking soda and salt. Add to banana mixture and stir in pecans. Mix well.
Step 4

Pour into prepared loaf pan and bake 1 hour and 20 minutes or until a cake tester inserted in the center comes out clean.
Nutrition Facts

Per Serving:

306.8 calories; protein 3.8g 8% DV; carbohydrates 44.2g 14% DV; fat 13.6g 21% DV; cholesterol 31.3mg 10% DV; sodium 221.1mg 9% DV.

Downeast Maine Pumpkin Bread

Prep: 15 mins **Cook:** 50 mins **Total:** 1 hr 5 mins **Servings:** 24 **Yield:** 3 - 7x3 inch loaf pans

Ingredients

- 1 (15 ounce) can pumpkin puree
- 4 large eggs eggs
- 1 cup vegetable oil
- ⅔ cup water
- 3 cups white sugar
- 3 ½ cups all-purpose flour
- 2 teaspoons baking soda
- 1 ½ teaspoons salt
- 1 teaspoon ground cinnamon
- 1 teaspoon ground nutmeg
- ½ teaspoon ground cloves
- ¼ teaspoon ground ginger

Directions

Step 1

Preheat oven to 350 degrees F (175 degrees C). Grease and flour three 7x3 inch loaf pans.

Step 2

In a large bowl, mix together pumpkin puree, eggs, oil, water and sugar until well blended. In a separate bowl, whisk together the flour, baking soda, salt, cinnamon, nutmeg, cloves and ginger. Stir the dry ingredients into the pumpkin mixture until just blended. Pour into the prepared pans.

Step 3

Bake for about 50 minutes in the preheated oven. Loaves are done when toothpick inserted in center comes out clean.

Nutrition Facts

Per Serving:

263.2 calories; protein 3.1g 6% DV; carbohydrates 40.6g 13% DV; fat 10.3g 16% DV; cholesterol 31mg 10% DV; sodium 305.4mg 12% DV.

Easy Fried Eggplant

Prep: 20 mins **Cook:** 15 mins **Total:** 35 mins **Servings:** 4 **Yield:** 4 servings

Ingredients

- 2 tablespoons canola oil
- 1 large eggplant, peeled and sliced
- 3 large eggs eggs, beaten
- 2 cups dry bread crumbs

Directions

Step 1

Heat oil in a large skillet over medium-high heat. Dip eggplant slices in egg, then in crumbs, and place in hot oil. Fry 2 to 3 minutes on each side, or until golden brown. Drain on paper towels.

Nutrition Facts

Per Serving:

357.1 calories; protein 13g 26% DV; carbohydrates 45.8g 15% DV; fat 13.8g 21% DV; cholesterol 139.5mg 47% DV; sodium 451mg 18% DV.

Corn Fritters

Prep: 10 mins **Cook:** 20 mins **Total:** 30 mins **Servings:** 12 **Yield:** 1 dozen fritters

Ingredients

- 3 cups oil for frying
- 1 cup sifted all-purpose flour
- 1 teaspoon baking powder
- ½ teaspoon salt
- ¼ teaspoon white sugar
- 1 egg, lightly beaten
- ½ cup milk
- 1 tablespoon shortening, melted
- 1 (12 ounce) can whole kernel corn, drained

Directions

Step 1

Heat oil in a heavy pot or deep fryer to 365 degrees F (185 degrees C).

Step 2

In a medium bowl, combine flour, baking powder, salt and sugar. Beat together egg, milk, and melted shortening; stir into flour mixture. Mix in the corn kernels.

Step 3

Drop fritter batter by spoonfuls into the hot oil, and fry until golden. Drain on paper towels.

Nutrition Facts

Per Serving:

132.7 calories; protein 2.7g 6% DV; carbohydrates 14g 5% DV; fat 7.8g 12% DV; cholesterol 17.5mg 6% DV; sodium 224.5mg 9% DV.

Apple Turnovers

Prep: 30 mins **Cook:** 25 mins **Total:** 55 mins **Servings:** 8 **Yield:** 8 turnovers

Ingredients

- 2 tablespoons lemon juice
- 4 cups water
- 4 eaches Granny Smith apples - peeled, cored and sliced
- 2 tablespoons butter
- 1 cup brown sugar
- 1 teaspoon ground cinnamon
- 1 tablespoon cornstarch
- 1 tablespoon water
- 1 (17.25 ounce) package frozen puff pastry sheets, thawed
- 1 cup confectioners' sugar
- 1 tablespoon milk
- 1 teaspoon vanilla extract

Directions

Step 1

Combine the lemon and 4 cups water in a large bowl. Place the sliced apples in the water to keep them from browning.

Step 2

Melt butter in a large skillet over medium heat. Drain water from apples, and place them into the hot skillet. Cook and stir for about 2 minutes. Add brown sugar, and cinnamon, and cook, stirring, for 2 more minutes. Stir together cornstarch and 1 tablespoon water. Pour into the skillet, and mix well. Cook for another minute, or until sauce has thickened. Remove from heat to cool slightly.

Step 3

Preheat the oven to 400 degrees F (200 degrees C).

Step 4

Unfold puff pastry sheets, and repair any cracks by pressing them back together. Trim each sheet into a square. Then cut each larger square into 4 smaller squares. Spoon apples onto the center of each squares. Fold over from corner to corner into a triangle shape, and press edges together to seal. Place turnovers on a baking sheet, leaving about 1 inch between them.

Step 5

Bake for 25 minutes in the preheated oven, until turnovers are puffed and lightly browned. Cool completely before glazing.

Step 6

To make the glaze, mix together the confectioners' sugar, milk and vanilla in a small bowl. Adjust the thickness by adding more sugar or milk if necessary. Drizzle glaze over the cooled turnovers.

Note

If you do not wish to make the glaze, you can brush beaten egg over the top of each turnover, and sprinkle with white sugar before baking.

Nutrition Facts

Per Serving:

561.9 calories; protein 4.8g 10% DV; carbohydrates 80g 26% DV; fat 25.9g 40% DV; cholesterol 7.8mg 3% DV; sodium 183.9mg 7% DV.

Cedar Planked Salmon

Prep: 15 mins **Cook:** 20 mins **Total:** 35 mins **Servings:** 6 **Yield:** 6 servings

Ingredients

- 3 (12 inch) untreated cedar planks
- ⅓ cup vegetable oil
- 1 ½ tablespoons rice vinegar
- 1 teaspoon sesame oil
- ⅓ cup soy sauce
- ¼ cup chopped green onions
- 1 tablespoon grated fresh ginger root
- 1 teaspoon minced garlic
- 2 (2 pound) salmon fillets, skin removed

Directions

Step 1

Soak the cedar planks for at least 1 hour in warm water. Soak longer if you have time.

Step 2

In a shallow dish, stir together the vegetable oil, rice vinegar, sesame oil, soy sauce, green onions, ginger, and garlic. Place the salmon fillets in the marinade and turn to coat. Cover and marinate for at least 15 minutes, or up to one hour.

Step 3

Preheat an outdoor grill for medium heat. Place the planks on the grate. The boards are ready when they start to smoke and crackle just a little.

Step 4

Place the salmon fillets onto the planks and discard the marinade. Cover, and grill for about 20 minutes. Fish is done when you can flake it with a fork. It will continue to cook after you remove it from the grill.

Nutrition Facts

Per Serving:

678.4 calories; protein 61.3g 123% DV; carbohydrates 1.7g 1% DV; fat 45.8g 70% DV; cholesterol 178.6mg 60% DV; sodium 981.2mg 39% DV.

Butternut Squash Soup II

Prep: 25 mins **Cook:** 45 mins **Total:** 1 hr 10 mins **Servings:** 4 **Yield:** 4 servings

Ingredients

- 2 tablespoons butter
- 1 small onion, chopped
- 1 stalk celery, chopped
- 1 medium carrot, chopped
- 2 medium potatoes, cubed
- 1 medium butternut squash - peeled, seeded, and cubed
- 1 (32 fluid ounce) container chicken stock
- 1 pinch salt and freshly ground black pepper to taste

Directions

Step 1

Melt the butter in a large pot, and cook the onion, celery, carrot, potatoes, and squash 5 minutes, or until lightly browned. Pour in enough of the chicken stock to cover vegetables. Bring to a boil. Reduce heat to low, cover pot, and simmer 40 minutes, or until all vegetables are tender.

Step 2

Transfer the soup to a blender, and blend until smooth. Return to pot, and mix in any remaining stock to attain desired consistency. Season with salt and pepper.

Nutrition Facts

Per Serving:

305.1 calories; protein 6.9g 14% DV; carbohydrates 59.7g 19% DV; fat 6.8g 11% DV; cholesterol 20.9mg 7% DV; sodium 1151.4mg 46% DV.

Beet Salad with Goat Cheese

Prep: 10 mins **Cook:** 30 mins **Total:** 40 mins **Servings:** 6 **Yield:** 6 servings

Ingredients

- 4 medium beets - scrubbed, trimmed and cut in half
- ⅓ cup chopped walnuts
- 3 tablespoons maple syrup
- 1 (10 ounce) package mixed baby salad greens
- ½ cup frozen orange juice concentrate
- ¼ cup balsamic vinegar
- ½ cup extra-virgin olive oil
- 2 ounces goat cheese

Directions

Step 1

Place beets into a saucepan, and fill with enough water to cover. Bring to a boil, then cook for 20 to 30 minutes, until tender. Drain and cool, then cut in to cubes.

Step 2

While the beets are cooking, place the walnuts in a skillet over medium-low heat. Heat until warm and starting to toast, then stir in the maple syrup. Cook and stir until evenly coated, then remove from the heat and set aside to cool.

Step 3

In a small bowl, whisk together the orange juice concentrate, balsamic vinegar and olive oil to make the dressing.

Step 4

Place a large helping of baby greens onto each of four salad plates, divide candied walnuts equally and sprinkle over the greens. Place equal amounts of beets over the greens, and top with dabs of goat cheese. Drizzle each plate with some of the dressing.

Nutrition Facts

Per Serving:

347.5 calories; protein 5.3g 11% DV; carbohydrates 25g 8% DV; fat 26.1g 40% DV; cholesterol 7.5mg 3% DV; sodium 107.5mg 4% DV.

Canned Apple Pie Filling

Servings: 56 Yield: 7 quarts

Ingredients

- 4 ½ cups white sugar
- 1 cup cornstarch
- 2 teaspoons ground cinnamon
- ¼ teaspoon ground nutmeg
- 2 teaspoons salt
- 10 cups water
- 3 tablespoons lemon juice
- 2 drops yellow food coloring
- 6 pounds apples

Directions

Step 1

in a large pan, mix sugar, cornstarch, cinnamon and nutmeg. Add salt and water and mix well. Bring to a boil and cook until thick and bubbly. Remove from heat and add lemon juice and food coloring.

Step 2

Sterilize canning jars, lids and rings by boiling them in a large pot of water.

Step 3

Peel, core, and slice apples. Pack the sliced apples into hot canning jars, leaving a 1/2 inch headspace.

Step 4

Fill jars with hot syrup, and gently remove air bubbles with a knife.

Step 5

Put lids on and process in a water bath canner for 20 minutes.

Nutrition Facts

Per Serving:

96.7 calories; protein 0.1g; carbohydrates 25g 8% DV; fat 0.1g; cholesterolmg; sodium 85mg 3% DV.

Pumpkin Spice

Prep: 2 mins Total: 2 mins Servings: 2 Yield: 2 teaspoons

Ingredients

- 1 teaspoon ground cinnamon
- ¼ teaspoon ground nutmeg
- ¼ teaspoon ground ginger
- ⅛ teaspoon ground cloves

Directions

Step 1

In a small bowl, mix together cinnamon, nutmeg, ginger and cloves. Store in an airtight container.

Nutrition Facts

Per Serving:

6 calories; protein 0.1g; carbohydrates 1.4g; fat 0.2g; cholesterolmg; sodium 0.6mg.

Cheese Fondue

Servings: 5 **Yield:** 5 servings

Ingredients

- 1 cup dry white wine
- ½ pound shredded Swiss cheese
- ½ pound shredded Gruyere cheese
- 2 tablespoons all-purpose flour
- ¼ teaspoon salt
- ¼ teaspoon ground nutmeg
- 1 (1 pound) loaf French bread, cut into 1 inch cubes

Directions

Step 1

Simmer wine in fondue pot. Add Swiss cheese, Gruyere cheese, 1/4 pound at a time. Stir after each addition of cheese until melted. Stir in flour. When all the cheese has melted, stir in salt and nutmeg. Serve with cut-up French bread.

Nutrition Facts

Per Serving:

669.8 calories; protein 36.5g 73% DV; carbohydrates 56.9g 18% DV; fat 28.9g 44% DV; cholesterol 91.2mg 30% DV; sodium 939.8mg 38% DV.

Peach Preserves

Prep: 20 mins **Cook:** 1 hr **Additional:** 40 mins **Total:** 2 hrs **Servings:** 64 **Yield:** 8 cups

Ingredients

- 12 medium (2-1/2" dia) (approx 4 per lb)s fresh peaches, pitted and chopped
- 4 ½ cups white sugar
- 1 (2 ounce) package dry pectin

Directions

Step 1

Crush 1 cup chopped peaches in the bottom of a large saucepan. Add remaining peaches, and set pan over medium-low heat. Bring to a low boil, and cook for about 20 minutes or until peaches become liquid (my family likes a few bits of peach left) .
Step 2

Pour peaches into a bowl, and then measure 6 cups back into the pan. Add sugar, and bring to a boil over medium heat. Gradually stir in dry pectin, and boil for 1 minute.
Step 3

Remove from heat after 1 minute, and transfer to sterilized jars. Process in hot water bath canner for 10 minutes. Let cool, and place on shelf.
Cook's Note:
When making preserves and jams, select slightly underipe, firm fruit .
Nutrition Facts
Per Serving:
59.1 calories; proteing; carbohydrates 15.2g 5% DV; fatg; cholesterolmg; sodium 0.7mg.

Banana-Zucchini Bread

Prep: 15 mins **Cook:** 50 mins **Total:** 1 hr 5 mins **Servings:** 20 **Yield:** 2 loaves

Ingredients

- 3 large eggs eggs
- ¾ cup vegetable oil
- ⅔ cup packed brown sugar
- 1 cup white sugar
- 1 cup grated zucchini
- 2 medium (7" to 7-7/8" long)s bananas, mashed
- 2 teaspoons vanilla extract
- 3 ½ cups all-purpose flour
- 1 tablespoon ground cinnamon
- 1 ½ teaspoons baking powder
- 1 teaspoon baking soda
- 1 teaspoon salt
- ½ cup dried cranberries
- ½ cup chopped walnuts

Directions
Step 1

Preheat oven to 325 degrees F (165 degrees C). Grease and flour two 8x4 inch bread loaf pans.
Step 2

In a large bowl, beat eggs until light yellow and frothy. Add oil, brown sugar, white sugar, grated zucchini, bananas, and vanilla; blend together until well combined. Stir in the flour, cinnamon, baking powder, baking soda, and salt. Mix in the cranberries and nuts. Divide the batter evenly between the two prepared loaf pans.

Step 3

Bake in the preheated oven until a toothpick inserted in the center comes out clean, about 50 minutes. Allow to cool in the loaf pans on a wire rack before removing and serving.

Nutrition Facts

Per Serving:

271.6 calories; protein 3.9g 8% DV; carbohydrates 40.2g 13% DV; fat 11.1g 17% DV; cholesterol 27.9mg 9% DV; sodium 229.6mg 9% DV.

Apple Pie Filling

Servings: 40 **Yield:** 5 - 9 inch pies

Ingredients

- 18 cups thinly sliced apples
- 3 tablespoons lemon juice
- 10 cups water
- 4 ½ cups white sugar
- 1 cup cornstarch
- 2 teaspoons ground cinnamon
- 1 teaspoon salt
- ¼ teaspoon ground nutmeg

Directions

Step 1

In a large bowl, toss apples with lemon juice and set aside. Pour water into a Dutch oven over medium heat. Combine sugar, cornstarch, cinnamon, salt, and nutmeg in a bowl; add to water, stir well, and bring to a boil. Boil for 2 minutes, stirring constantly.

Step 2

Add apples and return to a boil. Reduce heat, cover and simmer until apples are tender, about 6 to 8 minutes. Cool for 30 minutes.

Step 3

Ladle into 5 freezer containers, leaving 1/2 inch headspace. Cool at room temperature no longer than 1 1/2 hours.

Step 4

Seal and freeze. Can be stored for up to 12 months.

Nutrition Facts

Per Serving:

129.2 calories; protein 0.2g; carbohydrates 33.4g 11% DV; fat 0.1g; cholesterolmg; sodium 60.8mg 2% DV

Country Style Green Beans with Red Potatoes

Prep: 20 mins **Cook:** 3 hrs **Total:** 3 hrs 20 mins **Servings:** 8 **Yield:** 8 servings

Ingredients

- ½ pound smoked turkey tails
- 2 (14.5 ounce) cans green beans, drained and rinsed
- 1 large onion, chopped
- 10 small red potatoes, peeled and cubed
- 1 tablespoon seasoned salt
- 2 teaspoons ground black pepper
- 1 tablespoon garlic powder

Directions

Step 1

Place the turkey tails and onion into a 4 quart Dutch oven and fill half way full with water. Season with salt, pepper and garlic powder. Bring to a boil, then cover and simmer over low heat until meat falls off the bones, about 2 hours. Remove the bones and skin; return the meat to the pot. Discard bones and skin.

Step 2

Add the green beans to the Dutch oven and simmer for 20 minutes, then add the potatoes. Simmer for 10 to 15 minutes more, or until they can be easily pierced with a fork.

Nutrition Facts

Per Serving:

231.5 calories; protein 10.7g 21% DV; carbohydrates 42g 14% DV; fat 3.1g 5% DV; cholesterol 16.2mg 5% DV; sodium 935mg 37% DV.

Fondant Potatoes

Prep: 15 mins **Cook:** 40 mins **Additional:** 5 mins **Total:** 1 hr **Servings:** 6 **Yield:** 6 servings

Ingredients

- 3 large whole russet potatoes
- 2 tablespoons high-heat-resistant vegetable oil, such as grapeseed oil
- 1 pinch salt and ground black pepper to taste
- 3 tablespoons butter
- 4 sprigs thyme, plus more for garnish

- ½ cup chicken broth, or more as needed

Directions

Step 1

Preheat oven to 425 degrees F (220 degrees C).

Step 2

Cut off ends of russet potatoes, stand potatoes on end, and peel potatoes from top to bottom with a sharp knife to make each potato into a uniform cylinder. Cut each cylinder in half crosswise to make 6 potato cylinders about 2 inches long.

Step 3

Place potatoes into a bowl of cold water for about 5 minutes to remove starch from outsides; pat dry with paper towels.

Step 4

Place a heavy oven-proof skillet (such as a cast iron skillet) over high heat. Pour in vegetable oil; heat oil until it shimmers slightly.

Step 5

Place potato cylinders with best-looking ends into the hot oil, lower heat to medium-high, and pan-fry potatoes until well-browned, 5 to 6 minutes. Season with salt and black pepper.

Step 6

Flip the potatoes onto the opposite ends. As they cook, use a paper towel held with tongs to carefully blot out the oil from the skillet. Add butter and thyme sprigs to skillet.

Step 7

Pick up a thyme sprig with tongs and use it to paint butter over the top of the potatoes. Cook until butter foams and foam turns from white to a pale tan color. Season with more salt and pepper. Pour chicken stock into skillet.

Step 8

Transfer skillet to preheated oven and cook until potatoes are tender and creamy inside, about 30 minutes. If potatoes aren't tender, add 1/4 cup more stock and let cook 10 more minutes.

Step 9

Place potatoes on a serving platter and spoon thyme-scented butter remaining in skillet over potatoes. Garnish with thyme sprigs. Let cool about 5 minutes before serving.

Nutrition Facts

Per Serving:

238.5 calories; protein 4.1g 8% DV; carbohydrates 33.5g 11% DV; fat 10.5g 16% DV; cholesterol 15.8mg 5% DV; sodium 173mg 7% DV.

Quick Yeast Rolls

Prep: 1 hr 30 mins **Cook:** 10 mins **Total:** 1 hr 40 mins **Servings:** 8 **Yield:** 8 rolls

Ingredients

- 2 tablespoons shortening
- 3 tablespoons white sugar
- 1 cup hot water
- 1 (.25 ounce) package active dry yeast
- 1 egg, beaten
- 1 teaspoon salt
- 2 ¼ cups all-purpose flour

Directions

Step 1

In a large bowl, mix the shortening, sugar, and hot water. Allow to cool until lukewarm, and mix in the yeast until dissolved. Mix in the egg, salt, and flour. Allow the dough to rise until doubled in size.

Step 2

Grease 8 muffin cups. Divide the dough into the prepared muffin cups, and allow to rise again until doubled in size.

Step 3

Preheat oven to 425 degrees F (220 degrees C).

Step 4

Bake for 10 minutes in the preheated oven, or until a knife inserted in the center of a muffin comes out clean.

Nutrition Facts

Per Serving:

185.9 calories; protein 4.8g 10% DV; carbohydrates 31.9g 10% DV; fat 4.2g 7% DV; cholesterol 23.3mg 8% DV; sodium 301.5mg 12% DV.

Grilled Pork Loin Chops

Prep: 10 mins **Cook:** 25 mins **Additional:** 4 hrs **Total:** 4 hrs 35 mins **Servings:** 2 **Yield:** 2 servings

Ingredients

- 2 cloves garlic, minced
- 2 tablespoons brown sugar
- 3 tablespoons honey
- 3 tablespoons soy sauce
- 3 tablespoons Worcestershire sauce

- 2 teaspoons ketchup
- ½ teaspoon ground ginger
- ½ teaspoon onion powder
- ¼ teaspoon ground cinnamon
- ⅛ teaspoon cayenne pepper
- 2 (6 ounce) thick-cut boneless pork loin chops

Directions

Step 1

Mix the garlic, brown sugar, honey, soy sauce, Worcestershire sauce, ketchup, ginger, onion powder, cinnamon, and cayenne pepper together in a bowl. Pour half the mixture into a large plastic zipper bag, and place the pork chops into the marinade. Squeeze the air out of the bag, and seal the bag. Refrigerate 4 to 8 hours, turning occasionally. Refrigerate remaining marinade in the bowl.

Step 2

Preheat an outdoor grill for medium heat, and lightly oil the grate.

Step 3

Remove the pork chops from the plastic bag, and shake excess droplets of liquid from the chops. Discard the marinade from the plastic bag. Grill chops on the preheated grill, basting with the reserved marinade until meat is browned, no longer pink inside, and shows good grill marks, 8 to 10 minutes per side. A meat thermometer inserted into the thickest part of a chop should read at least 145 degrees F (63 degrees C).

Step 4

Pour remaining reserved marinade into a saucepan over medium heat, bring to a boil, and reduce heat to a simmer. Cook the marinade until slightly thickened, about 5 minutes, stirring constantly; serve sauce with chops.

Cook's Notes

Teriyaki sauce can replace the Worcestershire sauce with equally great results.

If thick enough, the chops can be cut into kabob sizes and marinated in the fridge for about two hours. Put on skewers with veggies of choice, and turn and baste as needed on a medium-temperature grill until done.

Nutrition Facts

Per Serving:

429 calories; protein 39.5g 79% DV; carbohydrates 49.3g 16% DV; fat 8.4g 13% DV; cholesterol 97.9mg 33% DV; sodium 1725.7mg 69% DV.

Two Ingredient Pumpkin Cake

Prep: 5 mins **Cook:** 25 mins **Total:** 30 mins **Servings:** 15 **Yield:** 1 - 9x13 inch cake

Ingredients

- 1 (18.25 ounce) package spice cake mix

- 1 (15 ounce) can pumpkin

Directions

Step 1

Preheat the oven to 350 degrees F (175 degrees C). Generously grease a 9x13 inch baking pan.

Step 2

In a large bowl, mix together the spice cake mix and canned pumpkin until well blended. Spread evenly into the prepared pan.

Step 3

Bake for 25 to 30 minutes in the preheated oven, or until a knife inserted into the center comes out clean. Cool and serve, or store in the refrigerator. This tastes even better the next day.

Nutrition Facts

Per Serving:

156.8 calories; protein 2.4g 5% DV; carbohydrates 27.5g 9% DV; fat 4.3g 7% DV; cholesterolmg; sodium 300.4mg 12% DV.

Baked Oatmeal II

Prep: 10 mins **Cook:** 40 mins **Total:** 50 mins **Servings:** 8 **Yield:** 8 servings

Ingredients

- 3 cups rolled oats
- 1 cup brown sugar
- 2 teaspoons ground cinnamon
- 2 teaspoons baking powder
- 1 teaspoon salt
- 1 cup milk
- 2 large eggs eggs
- ½ cup melted butter
- 2 teaspoons vanilla extract
- ¾ cup dried cranberries

Directions

Step 1

Preheat oven to 350 degrees F (175 degrees C).

Step 2

In a large bowl, mix together oats, brown sugar, cinnamon, baking powder, and salt. Beat in milk, eggs, melted butter, and vanilla extract. Stir in dried cranberries. Spread into a 9x13 inch baking dish.

Step 3

Bake in preheated oven for 40 minutes.

Nutrition Facts

Per Serving:

393.2 calories; protein 6.8g 14% DV; carbohydrates 59.2g 19% DV; fat 15.3g 24% DV; cholesterol 79.4mg 27% DV; sodium 502mg 20% DV.

Apple Pie I

Prep: 20 mins **Cook:** 40 mins **Total:** 1 hr **Servings:** 8 **Yield:** 1 pie

Ingredients

- 6 cups thinly sliced apples
- ¾ cup white sugar
- 1 tablespoon butter
- 1 teaspoon ground cinnamon
- 1 recipe pastry for a 9-inch double-crust pie

Directions

Step 1

Prepare your pastry for a two crust pie. Wipe, quarter, core, peel, and slice apples; measure to 6 cups.

Step 2

Combine sugar and cinnamon. The amount of sugar used depends on how tart your apples are.

Step 3

Arrange apples in layers in pastry lined pie plate. Sprinkle each layer with sugar and cinnamon. Dot top layer with small pieces of butter or margarine. Cover with top crust.

Step 4

Place on lowest rack in oven preheated to 450 degrees F (230 degrees C). Bake for 10 minutes, then reduce oven temperature to 350 degrees F (175 degrees C). Bake for 30 to 35 minutes longer. Serve warm or cold.

Nutrition Facts

Per Serving:

248.5 calories; protein 1.7g 3% DV; carbohydrates 42.2g 14% DV; fat 9.1g 14% DV; cholesterol 3.8mg 1% DV; sodium 128.1mg 5% DV.

Napa Cabbage Salad

Prep: 15 mins **Cook:** 15 mins **Total:** 30 mins **Servings:** 6 **Yield:** 6 servings

Ingredients

- 1 head napa cabbage

- 1 bunch minced green onions
- ⅓ cup butter
- 1 (3 ounce) package ramen noodles, broken
- 2 tablespoons sesame seeds
- 1 cup slivered almonds
- ¼ cup cider vinegar
- ¾ cup vegetable oil
- ½ cup white sugar
- 2 tablespoons soy sauce

Directions

Step 1

Finely shred the head of cabbage; do not chop. Combine the green onions and cabbage in a large bowl, cover and refrigerate until ready to serve.

Step 2

Preheat oven to 350 degrees F (175 degrees C).

Step 3

Make the crunchies: Melt the butter in a pot. Mix the ramen noodles, sesame seeds and almonds into the pot with the melted butter. Spoon the mixture onto a baking sheet and bake the crunchies in the preheated 350 degrees F (175 degrees C) oven, turning often to make sure they do not burn. When they are browned remove them from the oven.

Step 4

Make the dressing: In a small saucepan, heat vinegar, oil, sugar, and soy sauce. Bring the mixture to a boil, let boil for 1 minute. Remove the pan from heat and let cool.

Step 5

Combine dressing, crunchies, and cabbage immediately before serving. Serve right away or the crunchies will get soggy.

Nutrition Facts

Per Serving:

631.5 calories; protein 9.2g 18% DV; carbohydrates 39.8g 13% DV; fat 51.3g 79% DV; cholesterol 27.1mg 9% DV; sodium 652.5mg 26% DV.

Pecan Pie Bars I

Prep: 20 mins **Cook:** 45 mins **Total:** 1 hr 5 mins **Servings:** 36 **Yield:** 3 dozen

Ingredients

- 3 cups all-purpose flour

- ½ cup white sugar
- ½ teaspoon salt
- 1 cup margarine
- 4 large eggs eggs
- 1 ½ cups light corn syrup
- 1 ½ cups white sugar
- 3 tablespoons margarine, melted
- 1 ½ teaspoons vanilla extract
- 2 ½ cups chopped pecans

Directions

Step 1

Preheat oven to 350 degrees F (175 degrees C). Lightly grease a 10x15 inch jellyroll pan.

Step 2

In a large bowl, stir together the flour, 1/2 cup sugar, and salt. Cut in 1 cup of margarine until mixture resembles coarse crumbs. Sprinkle the mixture evenly over the prepared pan, and press in firmly.

Step 3

Bake for 20 minutes in the preheated oven.

Step 4

While the crust is baking, prepare the filling. In a large bowl mix together the eggs, corn syrup, 1 1/2 cups sugar, 3 tablespoons margarine, and vanilla until smooth. Stir in the chopped pecans. Spread the filling evenly over the crust as soon as it comes out of the oven.

Step 5

Bake for 25 minutes in the preheated oven, or until set. Allow to cool completely on a wire rack before slicing into bars.

Nutrition Facts

Per Serving:

232.8 calories; protein 2.5g 5% DV; carbohydrates 30.7g 10% DV; fat 12g 18% DV; cholesterol 20.7mg 7% DV; sodium 117.5mg 5% DV.

Acorn Squash

Prep: 5 mins **Cook:** 1 hr **Total:** 1 hr 5 mins **Servings:** 2 **Yield:** 2 squash halves

Ingredients

- 1 medium acorn squash, halved and seeded
- 1 tablespoon butter
- 2 tablespoons brown sugar

Directions
Step 1

Preheat oven to 350 degrees F (175 degrees C).
Step 2

Turn acorn squash upside down onto a cookie sheet. Bake in a 350 degrees F (175 degrees C) oven until it begins to soften, approximately 30 to 45 minutes.
Step 3

Remove squash from the oven and turn onto a plate so that the flesh is facing upwards. Place butter and brown sugar into the squash, and place remaining squash over the other piece. Place squash in a baking dish (so the squash won't slide around too much) while baking.
Step 4

Place squash in the 350 degrees F (175 degrees C) oven and bake another 30 minutes.
Nutrition Facts
Per Serving:
188.7 calories; protein 1.8g 4% DV; carbohydrates 35.8g 12% DV; fat 6g 9% DV; cholesterol 15.3mg 5% DV; sodium 51.2mg 2% DV.

Homemade Apple Cider

Prep: 15 mins **Cook:** 3 hrs 20 mins **Additional:** 4 hrs **Total:** 7 hrs 35 mins **Servings:** 16 **Yield:** 1 gallon cider

Ingredients
- 10 eaches apples, quartered
- ¾ cup white sugar
- 1 tablespoon ground cinnamon
- 1 tablespoon ground allspice

Directions
Step 1

Place apples in a large stockpot and add enough water cover by at least 2 inches. Stir in sugar, cinnamon, and allspice. Bring to a boil. Boil, uncovered, for 1 hour. Cover pot, reduce heat, and simmer for 2 hours.
Step 2

Strain apple mixture though a fine mesh sieve. Discard solids. Drain cider again though a cheesecloth lined sieve. Refrigerate until cold.
Cook's Note
Cider may be frozen for longer storage.
Nutrition Facts

Aunt Mary's Eggplant Balls

Prep: 30 mins **Cook:** 30 mins **Additional:** 15 mins **Total:** 1 hr 15 mins **Servings:** 6 **Yield:** 18 balls

Ingredients

- 3 tablespoons olive oil
- 3 cloves garlic, minced
- 4 cups cubed eggplant, with peel
- 1 tablespoon water
- ½ cup grated Parmesan cheese
- 1 cup chopped fresh parsley
- 2 large eggs eggs, beaten
- ¾ cup dried bread crumbs

Directions

Step 1

Preheat oven to 350 degrees F (175 degrees C). Grease a baking sheet.

Step 2

Heat a medium skillet over medium heat. Pour in olive oil and saute garlic just until lightly browned. Mix in eggplant and water. Reduce heat to low and cover skillet. Allow eggplant to steam until soft, about 20 minutes. Place eggplant in a large bowl and allow to cool slightly.

Step 3

Mix cheese, parsley, eggs, and bread crumbs into eggplant. Stir with a wooden spoon or your hands until ingredients are thoroughly combined and mixture can be rolled into balls. Add more bread crumbs as needed to make mixture workable. Refrigerate mixture for 15 minutes, then roll into balls or form into patties.

Step 4

Place eggplant balls on prepared baking sheet. Bake in preheated oven for 30 minutes. Serve immediately.

Nutrition Facts

Per Serving:

200.8 calories; protein 7.7g 15% DV; carbohydrates 16.1g 5% DV; fat 12.1g 19% DV; cholesterol 53.5mg 18% DV; sodium 257mg 10% DV.

Ranch Oyster Crackers

Prep: 10 mins **Cook:** 20 mins **Additional:** 15 mins **Total:** 45 mins **Servings:** 20 **Yield:** 5 cups

Ingredients

- 1 (1 ounce) package Ranch-style dressing mix
- ½ teaspoon dried dill weed
- ¼ cup vegetable oil
- ¼ teaspoon lemon pepper
- ¼ teaspoon garlic powder
- 5 cups oyster crackers

Directions

Step 1

Preheat oven to 250 degrees F (120 degrees C).

Step 2

In a large bowl, combine the dressing mix, dill weed, vegetable oil, lemon pepper, and garlic powder. Add oyster crackers, and toss to coat. Spread evenly on a baking sheet.

Step 3

Bake for 15 to 20 minutes in the preheated oven, stirring gently after 10 minutes. Remove from oven, and allow to cool before serving.

Nutrition Facts

Per Serving:

137.3 calories; protein 1.9g 4% DV; carbohydrates 16.2g 5% DV; fat 7g 11% DV; cholesterolmg; sodium 558.2mg 22% DV.

Pumpkin Chocolate Chip Cookies III

Servings: 24 **Yield:** 2 dozen

Ingredients

- 1 cup canned pumpkin
- 1 cup white sugar
- ½ cup vegetable oil
- 1 egg
- 2 cups all-purpose flour
- 2 teaspoons baking powder
- 2 teaspoons ground cinnamon
- ½ teaspoon salt
- 1 teaspoon baking soda
- 1 teaspoon milk
- 1 tablespoon vanilla extract

- 2 cups semisweet chocolate chips
- ½ cup chopped walnuts

Directions

Step 1

Combine pumpkin, sugar, vegetable oil, and egg. In a separate bowl, stir together flour, baking powder, ground cinnamon, and salt. Dissolve the baking soda with the milk and stir in. Add flour mixture to pumpkin mixture and mix well.

Step 2

Add vanilla, chocolate chips and nuts.

Step 3

Drop by spoonful on greased cookie sheet and bake at 350 degrees F (175 degrees C) for approximately 10 minutes or until lightly brown and firm.

Nutrition Facts

Per Serving:

202.4 calories; protein 2.4g 5% DV; carbohydrates 26.6g 9% DV; fat 10.7g 17% DV; cholesterol 7.8mg 3% DV; sodium 170.9mg 7% DV.

Roquefort Pear Salad

Prep: 20 mins **Cook:** 10 mins **Total:** 30 mins **Servings:** 6 **Yield:** 6 Servings

Ingredients

- 1 head leaf lettuce, torn into bite-size pieces
- 3 large pear (approx 2 per lb)s pears - peeled, cored and chopped
- 5 ounces Roquefort cheese, crumbled
- 1 avocado - peeled, pitted, and diced
- ½ cup thinly sliced green onions
- ¼ cup white sugar
- ½ cup pecans
- ⅓ cup olive oil
- 3 tablespoons red wine vinegar
- 1 ½ teaspoons white sugar
- 1 ½ teaspoons prepared mustard
- 1 clove garlic, chopped
- ½ teaspoon salt
- 1 dash fresh ground black pepper to taste

Directions

Step 1

In a skillet over medium heat, stir 1/4 cup of sugar together with the pecans. Continue stirring gently until sugar has melted and caramelized the pecans. Carefully transfer nuts onto waxed paper. Allow to cool, and break into pieces.

Step 2

For the dressing, blend oil, vinegar, 1 1/2 teaspoons sugar, mustard, chopped garlic, salt, and pepper.

Step 3

In a large serving bowl, layer lettuce, pears, blue cheese, avocado, and green onions. Pour dressing over salad, sprinkle with pecans, and serve.

Nutrition Facts

Per Serving:

426.2 calories; protein 8g 16% DV; carbohydrates 33.1g 11% DV; fat 31.6g 49% DV; cholesterol 21.3mg 7% DV; sodium 654mg 26% DV.

Greek Lentil Soup (Fakes)

Prep: 20 mins **Cook:** 1 hr **Total:** 1 hr 20 mins **Servings:** 4 **Yield:** 4 servings

Ingredients

- 8 ounces brown lentils
- ¼ cup olive oil
- 1 tablespoon minced garlic
- 1 onion, minced
- 1 large carrot, chopped
- 1 quart water
- 1 pinch dried oregano
- 1 pinch crushed dried rosemary
- 2 eaches bay leaves
- 1 tablespoon tomato paste
- 1 pinch salt and ground black pepper to taste
- 1 teaspoon olive oil, or to taste
- 1 teaspoon red wine vinegar, or to taste

Directions

Step 1

Place lentils in a large saucepan; add enough water to cover by 1 inch. Bring water to a boil and cook until tender, about 10 minutes; drain.

Step 2

Heat olive oil in a saucepan over medium heat. Add garlic, onion, and carrot; cook and stir until the onion has softened and turned translucent, about 5 minutes. Pour in lentils, 1 quart water, oregano, rosemary, and bay leaves. Bring to a boil. Reduce heat to medium-low, cover, and simmer for 10 minutes.

Step 3

Stir in tomato paste and season with salt and pepper. Cover and simmer until the lentils have softened, 30 to 40 minutes, stirring occasionally. Add additional water if the soup becomes too thick. Drizzle with 1 teaspoon olive oil and red wine vinegar to taste.

Nutrition Facts
Per Serving:
357.4 calories; protein 15.5g 31% DV; carbohydrates 40.3g 13% DV; fat 15.5g 24% DV; cholesterolmg; sodium 56.9mg 2% DV.

Gramma's Apple Bread Pudding

Prep: 15 mins **Cook:** 45 mins **Total:** 1 hr **Servings:** 8 **Yield:** 8 servings

Ingredients
PUDDING

- 4 cups soft bread cubes
- ¼ cup raisins
- 2 cups peeled and sliced apples
- 1 cup brown sugar
- 1 ¾ cups milk
- ¼ cup margarine
- 1 teaspoon ground cinnamon
- ½ teaspoon vanilla extract
- 2 large eggs eggs, beaten

VANILLA SAUCE

- ¼ cup white sugar
- ¼ cup brown sugar
- ½ cup milk
- ½ cup margarine
- 1 teaspoon vanilla extract

Directions
Step 1

Preheat oven to 350 degrees F (175 degrees C). Grease a 7x11 inch baking dish.
Step 2

In a large bowl, combine bread, raisins, and apples. In a small saucepan over medium heat, combine 1 cup brown sugar, 1 3/4 cups milk, and 1/4 cup margarine. Cook and stir until margarine is melted. Pour over bread mixture in bowl.

Step 3

In a small bowl, whisk together cinnamon, 1/2 teaspoon vanilla, and eggs. Pour bread mixture into prepared dish, and pour egg mixture over bread.

Step 4

Bake in preheated oven 40 to 50 minutes, or until center is set and apples are tender.

Step 5

While pudding is baking, mix together sugar, 1/4 cup brown sugar, 1/2 cup milk, and 1/2 cup margarine in a saucepan. Bring to a boil, then remove from heat, and stir in 1 teaspoon vanilla. Serve over bread pudding.

Nutrition Facts

Per Serving:

430 calories; protein 5.6g 11% DV; carbohydrates 58.8g 19% DV; fat 20g 31% DV; cholesterol 52mg 17% DV; sodium 372mg 15% DV.

Chocolate Wave Zucchini Bread

Servings: 12 **Yield:** 1 loaf

Ingredients

- ⅓ cup shortening
- 1 ⅓ cups white sugar
- 2 large eggs eggs
- 1 ½ cups grated zucchini
- ⅓ cup water
- 1 teaspoon vanilla extract
- 1 ⅔ cups all-purpose flour
- 1 teaspoon baking soda
- ½ teaspoon salt
- ¼ teaspoon baking powder
- 1 teaspoon pumpkin pie spice
- ⅓ cup chopped walnuts
- 3 tablespoons unsweetened cocoa powder
- ⅓ cup mini semi-sweet chocolate chips

Directions

Step 1

Preheat oven to 350 degrees F (175 degrees C). Grease one 9 x 5 inch loaf pan.

Step 2

In a large bowl, cream shortening and sugar together. Mix in eggs. Add zucchini, water, and vanilla; stir. Blend in flour, baking soda, salt , baking powder, and pumpkin pie spice. Stir in nuts.

Step 3

Divide batter in half, and add cocoa powder and chocolate chips to one of the halves. Pour plain batter into bottom of the loaf pan. Pour chocolate batter on top of plain batter.

Step 4

Bake until wooden pick inserted into center comes out clean, about 1 hour. Cool 10 minutes, and remove from pan. Store in refrigerator.

Nutrition Facts

Per Serving:

262.7 calories; protein 4g 8% DV; carbohydrates 40.4g 13% DV; fat 10.5g 16% DV; cholesterol 31mg 10% DV; sodium 226.5mg 9% DV.

No Sugar Apple Pie

Servings: 8 **Yield:** 1 pie

Ingredients

- 2 (9 inch) pie shell
- 3 tablespoons cornstarch
- 1 tablespoon ground cinnamon
- 1 (12 fluid ounce) can unsweetened apple juice concentrate, thawed
- 6 cups sliced green apples

Directions

Step 1

Preheat oven to 350 degrees F (175 degrees C).

Step 2

In a small bowl whisk together cornstarch, cinnamon, and 1/3 cup of the apple juice concentrate. Set aside.

Step 3

In a large saucepan simmer apples with remaining apple juice concentrate until apples are tender, about 10 minutes. Stir in cornstarch mixture and continue to simmer until thickened. Remove from heat.

Step 4

Spoon apple mixture into pastry-lined pie plate. Cover with top crust. Seal and flute edges. Cut steam vents in top.

Step 5

Bake in preheated oven for 45 minutes, or until crust is golden brown.

Nutrition Facts

Per Serving:

307 calories; protein 1.9g 4% DV; carbohydrates 52.4g 17% DV; fat 10.7g 17% DV; cholesterolmg; sodium 218.2mg 9% DV.

Easy Apple Crisp

Servings: 12 **Yield:** 12 servings

Ingredients

- 6 medium (2-3/4" dia) (approx 3 per lb)s apple - peeled, cored and sliced
- 1 cup water
- 1 (18.25 ounce) package white cake mix
- 1 cup packed brown sugar
- 1 teaspoon ground cinnamon
- ½ cup butter, melted

Directions

Step 1

Preheat oven to 350 degrees F (175 degrees C). Lightly grease a 9x13 inch baking dish.

Step 2

Arrange apples in an even layer in bottom of baking dish. Pour water over apples.

Step 3

In a medium bowl mix together cake mix, brown sugar, and cinnamon. Stir in melted butter or margarine until ingredients are thoroughly blended; mixture will be crumbly. Sprinkle mixture over apples.

Step 4

Bake in preheated oven for 50 to 55 minutes.

Nutrition Facts

Per Serving:

355.2 calories; protein 2.2g 4% DV; carbohydrates 60.9g 20% DV; fat 12.4g 19% DV; cholesterol 20.3mg 7% DV; sodium 343.7mg 14% DV.

Apple Butter Spice Cake

Prep: 25 mins **Cook:** 40 mins **Total:** 1 hr 5 mins **Servings:** 12 **Yield:** 1 9x13-inch cake

Ingredients

Topping:

- 1 cup packed brown sugar
- 1 teaspoon ground cinnamon
- ½ teaspoon ground nutmeg
- ½ cup chopped pecans

Cake:

- 2 cups all-purpose flour
- 1 teaspoon baking powder
- 1 teaspoon baking soda
- ½ teaspoon salt
- ½ cup butter, room temperature
- 1 cup white sugar
- ¾ cup apple butter
- 1 teaspoon vanilla extract
- ½ cup whole bran cereal or wheat germ
- 1 cup sour cream
- 2 large eggs eggs, room temperature

Directions

Step 1

Preheat oven to 350 degrees F (175 degrees C). Grease a 9x13-inch pan.

Step 2

Prepare the topping by mixing together the brown sugar, cinnamon, nutmeg, and chopped pecans.

Step 3

Sift together the flour, baking powder, baking soda, and salt.

Step 4

Beat butter and sugar together in a large bowl with an electric mixer until light and fluffy; add eggs one at a time, thoroughly beating each egg into the butter mixture before adding the next. Add apple butter, vanilla, and wheat germ or bran cereal. Add sifted dry ingredients alternately with sour cream; mix well after each addition.

Step 5

Pour half the batter into the prepared pan; sprinkle with half of the topping. Pour remaining batter into pan and top with the rest of the topping.

Step 6

Bake in the preheated oven until a tester inserted in the center comes out clean, about 40 minutes.

Nutrition Facts

Per Serving:

398.9 calories; protein 4.5g 9% DV; carbohydrates 60.9g 20% DV; fat 16.1g 25% DV; cholesterol 59.8mg 20% DV; sodium 335.8mg 13% DV.

German Apple Pancake

Prep: 15 mins **Cook:** 20 mins **Additional:** 10 mins **Total:** 45 mins **Servings:** 4 **Yield:** 4 servings

Ingredients

- 4 large eggs eggs
- ½ cup unbleached all-purpose flour
- ½ teaspoon baking powder
- 1 tablespoon sugar
- 1 pinch salt
- 1 cup milk
- 1 teaspoon vanilla extract
- 2 tablespoons unsalted butter, melted
- ½ teaspoon ground nutmeg
- ¼ cup unsalted butter
- ½ cup white sugar, divided
- ½ teaspoon ground cinnamon
- ½ teaspoon ground nutmeg
- 1 large tart apple - peeled, cored and sliced

Directions

Step 1

In a large bowl, blend eggs, flour, baking powder, sugar and salt. Gradually mix in milk, stirring constantly. Add vanilla, melted butter and 1/2 teaspoon nutmeg. Let batter stand for 30 minutes or overnight.

Step 2

Preheat oven to 425 degrees F (220 degrees C).

Step 3

Melt butter in a 10 inch oven proof skillet, brushing butter up on the sides of the pan. In a small bowl, combine 1/4 cup sugar, cinnamon and 1/2 teaspoon nutmeg. Sprinkle mixture over the butter. Line the pan with apple slices. Sprinkle remaining sugar over apples. Place pan over medium-high heat until the mixture bubbles, then gently pour the batter mixture over the apples.

Step 4

Bake in preheated oven for 15 minutes. Reduce heat to 375 degrees F (190 degrees C) and bake for 10 minutes. Slide pancake onto serving platter and cut into wedges.

Tips

This recipe appeared in Allrecipes Magazine as "Strawberry Dutch Baby Pancake," and used strawberries instead of apples.

Nutrition Facts

Per Serving:

455.9 calories; protein 10.3g 21% DV; carbohydrates 51.5g 17% DV; fat 24g 37% DV; cholesterol 236.6mg 79% DV; sodium 182.2mg 7% DV.

Roasted Duck

Prep: 10 mins **Cook:** 2 hrs **Total:** 2 hrs 10 mins **Servings:** 4 **Yield:** 4 servings

Ingredients

- 2 teaspoons salt
- 2 teaspoons paprika
- 1 teaspoon black pepper
- 1 (5 pound) whole duck
- ½ cup melted butter

Directions

Step 1

Preheat oven to 375 degrees F (190 degrees C).

Step 2

Rub salt, pepper, and paprika into the skin of the duck. Place in a roasting pan.

Step 3

Roast duck in preheated oven for 1 hour. Spoon 1/4 cup melted butter over bird, and continue cooking for 45 more minutes. Spoon remaining 1/4 cup melted butter over duck, and cook for 15 more minutes, or until golden brown.

Nutrition Facts

Per Serving:

624.9 calories; protein 51.8g 104% DV; carbohydrates 1g; fat 45.1g 69% DV; cholesterol 280mg 93% DV; sodium 1538.1mg 62% DV.

Roasted Roma Tomatoes

Prep: 15 mins **Cook:** 15 mins **Total:** 30 mins **Servings:** 4 **Yield:** 4 servings

Ingredients

- 8 medium (blank)s roma (plum) tomatoes, cut in half and seeds removed
- ¼ cup extra-virgin olive oil
- 2 tablespoons chopped garlic

- 1 teaspoon chopped fresh parsley
- 1 teaspoon chopped fresh basil
- 1 teaspoon chopped fresh oregano
- 1 pinch salt and black pepper to taste
- ½ cup crumbled feta cheese

Directions

Step 1

Preheat an oven to 375 degrees F (190 degrees C).

Step 2

Mix together the tomatoes, olive oil, garlic, parsley, basil, oregano, and salt and pepper in a bowl, working the seasonings into the cavities of the tomatoes. Place the tomatoes, cut sides up, on a baking sheet, and sprinkle each tomato with about 1 tablespoon of feta cheese.

Step 3

Bake the tomatoes in the preheated oven until cooked but still firm, about 15 minutes.

Note

Instead of using feta, substitute smoked gouda cheese.

Nutrition Facts

Per Serving:

204.6 calories; protein 4g 8% DV; carbohydrates 7.1g 2% DV; fat 18.3g 28% DV; cholesterol 16.7mg 6% DV; sodium 216.4mg 9% DV.

Chef John's Easy Apple Pie

Prep: 30 mins **Cook:** 50 mins **Additional:** 1 hr **Total:** 2 hrs 20 mins **Servings:** 8 **Yield:** 1 9-inch pie

Ingredients

- 6 tablespoons unsalted butter
- ¼ cup white sugar
- ½ cup brown sugar
- 1 pinch salt
- ¼ teaspoon ground cinnamon
- ¼ cup water
- 1 (15 ounce) package double crust ready-to-use pie crust (such as Pillsbury)
- 4 large red apples, cored and thinly sliced

Directions

Step 1

Preheat oven to 425 degrees F (220 degrees C).

Step 2

Melt butter in saucepan over medium heat. Stir in white sugar, brown sugar, salt, cinnamon, and water. Bring the syrup to a boil, stirring constantly to dissolve sugar, then remove from heat.

Step 3

Unroll pie crusts, press one into a 9-inch pie dish, and place the apples into the crust. Unroll the second crust on a work surface, and cut into about 8 1-inch wide strips. Criss-cross the strips over the apples, or weave into a lattice crust. Crimp the bottom crust over the lattice strips with your fingers. Spoon caramel sauce over pie, covering lattice portion of top crust; let remaining sauce drizzle through the crust.

Step 4

Bake in preheated oven for 15 minutes. Reduce heat to 350 degrees F (175 degrees C), and bake until the crust is golden brown, the caramel on the top crust is set, and the apple filling is bubbling, 35 to 40 more minutes. Allow to cool completely before slicing.

Nutrition Facts

Per Serving:

454.3 calories; protein 3.4g 7% DV; carbohydrates 56.6g 18% DV; fat 25g 38% DV; cholesterol 22.9mg 8% DV; sodium 259.4mg 10% DV.

Asian Marinated Pork Chops

Prep: 10 mins **Cook:** 15 mins **Additional:** 30 mins **Total:** 55 mins **Servings:** 6 **Yield:** 6 servings

Ingredients

- 1 cup soy sauce
- ½ cup brown sugar
- 2 cloves garlic, crushed
- 1 tablespoon ground ginger
- 1 tablespoon ground cumin
- 1 tablespoon roasted red chili paste
- 6 (1-inch thick) pork chops

Directions

Step 1

Place the soy sauce, brown sugar, garlic, ginger, cumin, and chili paste in a large, heavy plastic zipper bag. Smush the bag a few times with your fingers to mix all the ingredients thoroughly and dissolve the brown sugar; place the pork chops into the marinade, and seal the bag. Allow to marinate for 30 to 45 minutes.

Step 2

Preheat an outdoor grill for medium heat, and lightly oil the grate.

Step 3

Remove the pork chops from the marinade, and discard the marinade. Shake off excess marinade, and grill the pork chops until browned, the meat is no longer pink inside, and the chops show good grill marks, 5 to 7 minutes per side. An instant-read meat thermometer inserted into the thickest part of a chop should read at least 145 degrees F (63 degrees C).

Nutrition Facts

Per Serving:

447.9 calories; protein 57.4g 115% DV; carbohydrates 24.1g 8% DV; fat 12.6g 19% DV; cholesterol 142.1mg 47% DV; sodium 2522.9mg 101% DV.

Mexican Pumpkin Empanadas

Prep: 40 mins **Cook:** 20 mins **Total:** 1 hr **Servings:** 12 **Yield:** 12 empanadas

Ingredients

- 3 cups all-purpose flour
- ⅓ cup white sugar
- 1 ½ teaspoons salt
- ¼ teaspoon baking powder
- 1 cup vegetable shortening
- 1 cup warm water
- 4 cups canned pure pumpkin
- 2 large eggs eggs
- 1 cup white sugar
- 1 teaspoon salt
- 1 ½ teaspoons ground cinnamon
- 1 teaspoon ground ginger
- ½ teaspoon ground cloves
- 1 beaten egg

Directions

Step 1

Preheat oven to 350 degrees F (175 degrees C). Line baking sheets with parchment paper.

Step 2

In a large bowl, whisk the flour, 1/3 cup of sugar, 1 1/2 teaspoons of salt, and baking powder together. Cut the shortening into the flour mixture until it resembles coarse crumbs; stir the water in, about 2 tablespoons at a time, just until you can gather the dough together. Knead the dough a few times in the bowl, then scrape it out onto a floured surface. Cut the dough in quarters, and cut each quarter into thirds to make 12 equal portions. Roll the portions into balls. Cover the dough balls with a cloth, and allow to rest while you make the filling.

Step 3

Mix the pumpkin, 2 eggs, 1 cup of sugar, 1 teaspoon of salt, cinnamon, ginger, and cloves together until smooth. On a floured surface, roll each dough ball out into a thin circle about 6 inches across; spoon about 1/3 cup of filling into the center of the dough circle. Fold the dough over the filling to make a half-moon shaped pie, and crimp the edges of the crust together with a fork, leaving little fork lines in the dough. Gently lay the empanadas onto the prepared baking sheets. Brush the top of each pie with beaten egg.

Step 4

Bake in the preheated oven until the filling is hot and the crusts are shiny and browned, about 20 minutes.

Nutrition Facts

Per Serving:

384.2 calories; protein 5.5g 11% DV; carbohydrates 52.3g 17% DV; fat 18.6g 29% DV; cholesterol 46.5mg 16% DV; sodium 709.8mg 28% DV.

Instant Pot Chicken and Dumplings

Prep: 20 mins **Cook:** 25 mins **Additional:** 5 mins **Total:** 50 mins **Servings:** 5 **Yield:** 5 servings

Ingredients

- ½ tablespoon olive oil
- 1 cup diced onion
- ½ cup diced carrot
- ½ cup diced celery
- 1 bay leaf
- 4 cups low-sodium chicken broth
- 1 pound boneless, skinless chicken thighs
- 1 pound bone-in chicken breasts, skin removed
- ½ teaspoon thyme
- ½ teaspoon dried marjoram
- 1 teaspoon salt
- ¼ teaspoon freshly ground black pepper
- 2 tablespoons unsalted butter, softened
- 2 tablespoons all-purpose flour
- 1 pinch salt and ground black pepper to taste
- ½ cup frozen petite peas
- ½ cup frozen cut green beans

Dumplings:

- 1 cup all-purpose flour
- 1 teaspoon baking powder
- ½ teaspoon salt
- 2 tablespoons cold unsalted butter

- 1 tablespoon chopped fresh flat-leaf parsley
- ½ cup buttermilk

Directions

Step 1

Pour the olive oil into a multi-functional pressure cooker (such as an Instant Pot) and select the Saute function. Cook onion, carrot, celery, and bay leaf until the vegetables are soft and the onion has turned translucent, about 5 minutes.

Step 2

Add chicken broth, chicken thighs, chicken breasts, thyme, marjoram, salt, and pepper. Close and lock the lid. Select high pressure according to manufacturer's instructions; set timer for 9 minutes. Allow 10 to 15 minutes for pressure to build.

Step 3

Release pressure carefully using the quick-release method according to manufacturer's instructions, about 5 minutes. Carefully remove the chicken pieces with tongs and place them in a bowl to cool slightly; discard bay leaf.

Step 4

Mash butter with the flour to make a smooth paste; set aside.

Step 5

Combine flour, baking powder, and salt in a bowl for the dumplings. Cut in cold butter until mixture is the texture of cornmeal. Stir in parsley and set aside.

Step 6

Shred cooled chicken and return to the pot. Taste the broth and adjust the seasoning if needed. Add peas and green beans. Stir in the flour-butter paste. Select Saute function to bring broth back to a boil.

Step 7

Pour buttermilk into the dumpling mixture and stir until combined. Drop the dumpling dough by heaping spoonfuls on top of the stew; a small cookie scoop works well.

Step 8

Cover pot with the lid, leaving the steam vent open. Select Slow Cooker function and simmer on Low, covered, until dumplings are cooked through, 10 to 12 minutes. A skewer inserted in the center of a dumpling should come out clean.

Cook's Notes:

If you want to use this as a pot pie filling, decrease the chicken broth to 2 cups.

If you have a mini food processor, it's perfect for step 5. Transfer the flour-butter mixture to a bowl before proceeding.

Nutrition Facts

Pumpkin Roll I

Prep: 15 mins **Cook:** 25 mins **Additional:** 20 mins **Total:** 1 hr **Servings:** 10 **Yield:** 10 servings

Ingredients

- 3 large eggs eggs, beaten
- 1 cup white sugar
- ½ teaspoon ground cinnamon
- ⅔ cup pumpkin puree
- ¾ cup all-purpose flour
- 1 teaspoon baking soda
- 2 tablespoons butter, softened
- 8 ounces cream cheese
- 1 cup confectioners' sugar
- ¼ teaspoon vanilla extract
- 2 tablespoons confectioners' sugar for dusting

Directions

Step 1

Preheat oven to 375 degrees F (190 degrees C). Butter or grease one 10x15 inch jelly roll pan.

Step 2

In a mixing bowl, blend together the eggs, sugar, cinnamon, and pumpkin. In a separate bowl, mix together flour and baking soda. Add to pumpkin mixture and blend until smooth. Evenly spread the mixture over the prepared jelly roll pan.

Step 3

Bake 15 to 25 minutes in the preheated oven. Remove from oven and allow to cool enough to handle.

Step 4

Remove cake from pan and place on tea towel (cotton, not terry cloth). Roll up the cake by rolling a towel inside cake and place seam side down to cool.

Step 5

Prepare the frosting by blending together the butter, cream cheese, confectioners sugar, and vanilla.

Step 6

When cake is completely cooled, unroll and spread with cream cheese filling. Roll up again without towel. Wrap with plastic wrap and refrigerate until ready to serve. Sprinkle top with confectioners sugar and slice into 8-10 servings.

Nutrition Facts
Per Serving:
288.8 calories; protein 4.7g 9% DV; carbohydrates 42.2g 14% DV; fat 11.8g 18% DV; cholesterol 86.9mg 29% DV; sodium 230.9mg 9% DV.

Eggplant Parmesan I

Prep: 25 mins **Cook:** 45 mins **Additional:** 30 mins **Total:** 1 hr 40 mins **Servings:** 8 **Yield:** 8 servings

Ingredients

- 1 eggplant, cut into 3/4 inch slices
- 1 ½ tablespoons salt
- 8 tablespoons olive oil
- 8 ounces ricotta cheese
- 6 ounces shredded mozzarella cheese
- ½ cup grated Parmesan cheese
- 1 egg, beaten
- ½ cup chopped fresh basil
- 4 cups pasta sauce

Directions

Step 1

Sprinkle both sides of the eggplant slices with salt. Place slices in a colander, and place a dish underneath the colander to capture liquid that will sweat out of the eggplant. Allow to sit for 30 minutes.

Step 2

Preheat oven to 350 degrees F (175 degrees C). In a medium bowl, mix the ricotta, mozzarella cheese and 1/4 cup Parmesan cheese. Mix in egg and basil.

Step 3

Rinse the eggplant in cold water until all salt is removed. In a large skillet, heat 4 tablespoons olive oil over medium heat. Place one layer of eggplant in the pan, brown each side. Repeat with remaining eggplant slices, using additional oil if necessary.

Step 4

In a 9x13 inch baking dish, evenly spread 1 1/2 cups of spaghetti sauce. Arrange a single layer of eggplant slices on top of the sauce. Top the eggplant with 1/2 of the cheese mixture. Repeat layering process until all the eggplant and cheese mixture is used. Pour remaining sauce on top of layers, and sprinkle with remaining Parmesan cheese.

Step 5

Bake 30 to 45 minutes in the preheated oven, until sauce is bubbly.

Nutrition Facts

Per Serving:

368.8 calories; protein 14.1g 28% DV; carbohydrates 23.5g 8% DV; fat 24.7g 38% DV; cholesterol 52.5mg 18% DV; sodium 2074.6mg 83% DV.

Rachel's Cranberry Chicken Salad

Prep: 15 mins **Total:** 15 mins **Servings:,**4 **Yield:** 4 servings

Ingredients

- 2 breast half, bone and skin removed (blank)s cooked chicken breast halves, chopped
- ½ cup mayonnaise, or to taste
- 2 eaches green onions, chopped
- ½ cup sweetened dried cranberries (such as Ocean Spray Craisins)
- ¼ green apple, shredded
- ¼ cup chopped pecans
- 1 tablespoon lime juice
- 1 pinch salt and black pepper to taste
- ¼ teaspoon dried dill weed

Directions

Step 1

Mix together the chicken and mayonnaise in a bowl, stir to coat well, then stir in the green onions, dried cranberries, apple, pecans, lime juice, salt, pepper, and dill weed. Serve immediately, or refrigerate several hours or overnight (the flavor just gets better).

Cook's Note

Use 1 tablespoon fresh chopped dill instead of the dried dill.

Nutrition Facts

Per Serving:

384.2 calories; protein 14.1g 28% DV; carbohydrates 16.2g 5% DV; fat 30.3g 47% DV; cholesterol 46.1mg 15% DV; sodium 187.1mg 8% DV.

Cranberry Pistachio Biscotti

Prep: 25 mins **Cook:** 45 mins **Additional:** 10 mins **Total:** 1 hr 20 mins **Servings:** 36 **Yield:** 3 dozen

Ingredients

- ¼ cup light olive oil

- ¾ cup white sugar
- 2 teaspoons vanilla extract
- ½ teaspoon almond extract
- 2 large eggs eggs
- 1 ¾ cups all-purpose flour
- ¼ teaspoon salt
- 1 teaspoon baking powder
- ½ cup dried cranberries
- 1 ½ cups pistachio nuts

Directions

Step 1

Preheat the oven to 300 degrees F (150 degrees C).

Step 2

In a large bowl, mix together oil and sugar until well blended. Mix in the vanilla and almond extracts, then beat in the eggs. Combine flour, salt, and baking powder; gradually stir into egg mixture. Mix in cranberries and nuts by hand.

Step 3

Divide dough in half. Form two logs (12x2 inches) on a cookie sheet that has been lined with parchment paper. Dough may be sticky; wet hands with cool water to handle dough more easily.

Step 4

Bake for 35 minutes in the preheated oven, or until logs are light brown. Remove from oven, and set aside to cool for 10 minutes. Reduce oven heat to 275 degrees F (135 degrees C).

Step 5

Cut logs on diagonal into 3/4 inch thick slices. Lay on sides on parchment covered cookie sheet. Bake approximately 8 to 10 minutes, or until dry; cool.

Nutrition Facts

Per Serving:

91.8 calories; protein 2.1g 4% DV; carbohydrates 11.7g 4% DV; fat 4.3g 7% DV; cholesterol 10.3mg 3% DV; sodium 55.3mg 2% DV.

Easy Pumpkin Muffins

Prep: 5 mins **Cook:** 25 mins **Total:** 30 mins **Servings:** 12 **Yield:** 12 muffins

Ingredients

- 1 (18.25 ounce) package yellow cake mix
- 1 (15 ounce) can pumpkin puree

- 1 teaspoon ground cinnamon
- ½ teaspoon ground nutmeg
- ¼ teaspoon ground cloves

Directions

Step 1

Preheat the oven to 350 degrees F (175 degrees C). Grease a 12 cup muffin pan or line with paper liners.

Step 2

In a large bowl, mix together the cake mix, pumpkin puree, cinnamon, nutmeg and cloves until smooth. Spoon equal amounts of batter into the prepared muffin cups.

Step 3

Bake for 20 to 25 minutes in the preheated oven, until a toothpick inserted in the center of one comes out clean.

Nutrition Facts

Per Serving:

199.5 calories; protein 2.3g 5% DV; carbohydrates 36.8g 12% DV; fat 5.2g 8% DV; cholesterol 0.9mg; sodium 368.8mg 15% DV.

Chef John's Pumpkin Pie

Prep: 15 mins **Cook:** 45 mins **Total:** 1 hr **Servings:** 8 **Yield:** 1 9-inch pie

Ingredients

- 1 (15 ounce) can pumpkin puree
- 3 large egg yolks egg yolks
- 1 large egg
- 1 (14 ounce) can sweetened condensed milk
- 1 teaspoon ground cinnamon
- ½ teaspoon ground ginger
- ½ teaspoon fine salt
- ¼ teaspoon freshly grated nutmeg
- ⅛ teaspoon Chinese 5-spice powder
- 1 9-inch unbaked pie crust (see footnote for recipe link)

Directions

Step 1

Preheat oven to 425 degrees F (220 degrees C).

Step 2

Whisk together pumpkin puree, egg yolks, and egg in a large bowl until smooth. Add sweetened condensed milk, cinnamon, ginger, salt, nutmeg, and Chinese 5-spice powder; whisk until thoroughly combined.
Step 3

Fit pie crust in a 9-inch pie plate and crimp edges.
Step 4

Pour filling into the pie shell and lightly tap on the work surface to release any air bubbles.
Step 5

Bake in the preheated oven for 15 minutes.
Step 6

Reduce heat to 350 degrees F (175 degrees C) and bake until just set in the middle, 30 to 40 more minutes. A paring knife inserted into the filling, 1 inch from the crust, should come out clean. Allow to cool completely before serving.

Cook's Note:

If desired, substitute 1 small pinch of ground star anise, ground cloves, and ground white pepper for five-spice powder.

Nutrition Facts

Per Serving:

319.5 calories; protein 7.6g 15% DV; carbohydrates 41.9g 14% DV; fat 14.2g 22% DV; cholesterol 116.7mg 39% DV; sodium 464.6mg 19% DV.

Autumn Rainbow Sheet Pan Dinner

Prep: 15 mins **Cook:** 27 mins **Additional:** 1 hr **Total:** 1 hr 42 mins **Servings:** 6 **Yield:** 6 servings

Ingredients

- 3 large (blank)s chicken breasts, halved
- 1 (12 ounce) bottle garlic rosemary citrus marinade (such as Stonewall Kitchen
- ½ pound butternut squash, peeled and chopped
- ½ pound fresh brussels sprouts, halved
- ½ pound baby carrots
- 1 Gala apple - peeled, cored, and cut into 1/2-inch cubes
- 2 tablespoons olive oil
- 1 pinch salt and freshly ground black pepper to taste

Directions

Step 1

Place chicken breast halves in a gallon-size resealable plastic bag and add marinade. Refrigerate for 1 hour.
Step 2

Preheat oven to 450 degrees F (230 degrees C). Line a sheet pan with heavy-duty aluminum foil.

Step 3

Place butternut squash, brussels sprouts, baby carrots, and apple on the sheet pan. Drizzle with olive oil and sprinkle with salt and pepper. Place marinated chicken breasts on top of vegetable-fruit mixture and drizzle with leftover marinade from bag.

Step 4

Bake in the preheated oven until chicken is no longer pink and the juices run clear, 25 to 30 minutes. An instant-read thermometer inserted into the center should read 165 degrees F (74 degrees C). Turn on the oven's broiler. Broil until vegetables are lightly browned, 2 to 3 minutes.

Nutrition Facts

Per Serving:

342.3 calories; protein 43.2g 86% DV; carbohydrates 19.1g 6% DV; fat 9.5g 15% DV; cholesterol 112.9mg 38% DV; sodium 1114.5mg 45% DV.

Nana's Apple Crisp

Prep: 15 mins **Cook:** 50 mins **Total:** 1 hr 5 mins **Servings:** 8 **Yield:** 8 servings

Ingredients

- 6 medium (2-3/4" dia) (approx 3 per lb)s tart apples - peeled, cored, and sliced
- ½ cup butter, melted
- 1 cup all-purpose flour
- 1 cup white sugar
- 1 cup quick-cooking oats
- 2 tablespoons ground cinnamon, divided
- ¼ cup butter, cut into pieces

Directions

Step 1

Preheat oven to 350 degrees F (175 degrees C).

Step 2

Place apples in a 9x13 inch baking dish. In a bowl, mix melted butter, flour, sugar, oats, and 1 tablespoon cinnamon to form a crumbly mixture. Sprinkle over apples. Dot with remaining 1/4 cup butter, and sprinkle with remaining 1 tablespoon cinnamon.

Step 3

Bake 50 minutes in the preheated oven, until lightly browned and apples are tender.

Tips

The magazine version of this recipe uses 3/4 cup butter and bakes the crisp at 375 degrees F (190 degrees C) for 35 to 40 minutes.

Nutrition Facts

Per Serving:

402.7 calories; protein 3.5g 7% DV; carbohydrates 59.5g 19% DV; fat 18.3g 28% DV; cholesterol 45.8mg 15% DV; sodium 124.7mg 5% DV.

Eggplant Croquettes

Prep: 15 mins **Cook:** 20 mins **Total:** 35 mins **Servings:** 6 **Yield:** 6 servings

Ingredients

- 2 eggplant, peeled (yield from 1.25 lb)s medium eggplants, peeled and cubed
- 1 cup shredded sharp Cheddar cheese
- 1 cup Italian seasoned bread crumbs
- 2 large eggs eggs, beaten
- 2 tablespoons dried parsley
- 2 tablespoons chopped onion
- 1 clove garlic, minced
- 1 cup vegetable oil for frying
- 1 teaspoon salt
- ½ teaspoon ground black pepper

Directions

Step 1

Place eggplant in a microwave safe bowl and microwave on medium-high 3 minutes. Turn eggplant over and microwave another 2 minutes. The eggplant should be tender, cook another 2 minutes if the eggplants are not tender. Drain any liquid from the eggplants and mash.

Step 2

Combine cheese, bread crumbs, eggs, parsley, onion, garlic and salt with the mashed eggplant. Mix well.

Step 3

Shape the eggplant mixture into patties. Heat oil in a large skillet. Drop eggplant patties one at a time into skillet. Fry each side of the patties until golden brown, approximately 5 minutes on each side. Patties can be frozen before frying and cooked later.

Nutrition Facts

Per Serving:

265.9 calories; protein 12.4g 25% DV; carbohydrates 23.6g 8% DV; fat 14.4g 22% DV; cholesterol 86.3mg 29% DV; sodium 910.9mg 36% DV.

Apple Cake I

Servings: 24 **Yield:** 1 -9x13 inch cake

Ingredients

- 2 large eggs eggs
- 1 cup vegetable oil
- 2 cups white sugar
- 2 cups all-purpose flour
- 2 teaspoons ground cinnamon
- 1 teaspoon baking soda
- ½ teaspoon salt
- 1 teaspoon vanilla extract
- 4 cups diced apple without peel

Directions

Step 1

Preheat oven to 350 degrees F (175 degrees C). Lightly grease and flour one 9x13 inch cake pan.

Step 2

Beat vegetable oil and eggs until foamy. Add the sugar, flour, ground cinnamon, baking, soda, salt, and vanilla and mix well. Stir in the diced apples. Pour batter into prepared pan.

Step 3

Bake at 350 degrees F (175 degrees C) for 30 to 40 minutes. Cool cake in pan for 10 minutes. Cake needs no frosting.

Nutrition Facts

Per Serving:

201.2 calories; protein 1.7g 3% DV; carbohydrates 27.7g 9% DV; fat 9.7g 15% DV; cholesterol 15.5mg 5% DV; sodium 107.2mg 4% DV.

Pumpkin Spice Coffee Syrup

Prep: 10 mins **Cook:** 20 mins **Total:** 30 mins **Servings:** 16 **Yield:** 3 cups

Ingredients

- 1 ½ cups water
- 1 ½ cups white sugar
- ½ cup pumpkin pie filling, or to taste, divided
- 4 eaches cinnamon sticks
- 4 teaspoons freshly grated nutmeg

- 2 teaspoons minced fresh ginger
- 2 teaspoons whole cloves
- 2 teaspoons vanilla extract
- ½ teaspoon pumpkin pie spice
- ¼ cup sweetened condensed milk

Directions

Step 1

Mix water and sugar in a saucepan. Bring water to a boil, reduce heat to medium-low, and cook, stirring regularly, until sugar is dissolved completely into a simple syrup, about 5 minutes.

Step 2

Stir 6 tablespoons pumpkin pie filling, cinnamon sticks, nutmeg, ginger, cloves, vanilla extract, and pumpkin pie spice into the syrup. Bring liquid again to a simmer and cook until the syrup is well-spiced, 8 to 10 minutes.

Step 3

Strain the mixture through a sheet of cheesecloth. Return liquid to the saucepan over low heat.

Step 4

Stir sweetened condensed milk and remaining 2 tablespoons pumpkin pie filling into the spiced syrup and cook, stirring regularly, until the pumpkin dissolves into the liquid, about 5 minutes.

Cook's Notes:

Store in refrigerator for up to two weeks.

For a pumpkin spice latte: mix 3 tablespoons syrup with 1 to 2 shots brewed espresso and 3/4 cup steamed milk (2% for a fuller, creamier latte) in a mug.

Nutrition Facts

Per Serving:

104.5 calories; protein 0.6g 1% DV; carbohydrates 24.6g 8% DV; fat 0.7g 1% DV; cholesterol 1.6mg 1% DV; sodium 25.2mg 1% DV.

Apple Crisp III

Prep: 20 mins **Cook:** 40 mins **Total:** 1 hr **Servings:** 6 **Yield:** 6 servings

Ingredients

- 4 cups sliced apples
- 1 teaspoon ground cinnamon
- ½ cup water
- 1 cup white sugar
- ½ cup butter
- ¾ cup all-purpose flour

Directions

Step 1

Preheat oven to 350 degrees F (175 degrees C). Grease an 8x8 inch baking dish.

Step 2

Place apples in prepared dish. Sprinkle with cinnamon. Pour water over all. In a bowl, cream together sugar and butter. Blend in flour. Sprinkle mixture evenly over apples.

Step 3

Bake in preheated oven 30 to 40 minutes, until apples are tender and crust is golden.

Nutrition Facts

Per Serving:

360.6 calories; protein 2g 4% DV; carbohydrates 55.7g 18% DV; fat 15.6g 24% DV; cholesterol 40.7mg 14% DV; sodium 110.6mg 4% DV.

Applesauce

Prep: 20 mins **Cook:** 15 mins **Total:** 35 mins **Servings:** 4 **Yield:** 4 servings

Ingredients

- 6 cups apples - peeled, cored and chopped
- ¾ cup water
- ⅛ teaspoon ground cinnamon
- ⅛ teaspoon ground cloves
- ½ cup white sugar

Directions

Step 1

In a 2 quart saucepan over medium heat, combine apples, water, cinnamon, and cloves. Bring to a boil, reduce heat, and simmer 10 minutes. Stir in sugar, and simmer 5 more minutes.

Nutrition Facts

Per Serving:

194.6 calories; protein 0.5g 1% DV; carbohydrates 51g 16% DV; fat 0.3g 1% DV; cholesterolmg; sodium 2mg.

Dutch Apple Pie with Oatmeal Streusel

Servings: 8 **Yield:** 1 pie

Ingredients

- 1 (9 inch) pie shell

- 5 cups apples - peeled, cored and sliced
- 2 tablespoons all-purpose flour
- ⅔ cup white sugar
- ½ teaspoon ground cinnamon
- ¼ teaspoon ground nutmeg
- ¼ teaspoon ground allspice
- 2 tablespoons butter
- ¾ cup all-purpose flour
- ½ teaspoon ground cinnamon
- ½ cup packed brown sugar
- ¾ cup rolled oats
- 1 teaspoon lemon zest
- ½ cup butter

Directions

Step 1

Preheat oven to 425 degrees F (220 degrees C). Fit pastry shell into pie pan and place in freezer.

Step 2

To Make Apple Filling: Place apples in a large bowl. In a separate bowl combine 2 tablespoons flour, white sugar, 1/2 teaspoon cinnamon, nutmeg, and allspice. Mix well, then add to apples. Toss until apples are evenly coated.

Step 3

Remove pie shell from freezer. Place apple mixture in pie shell and dot with 2 tablespoons butter or margarine. Lay a sheet of aluminum foil lightly on top of filling, but do not seal.

Step 4

Bake in preheated oven for 10 minutes.

Step 5

While filling is baking, make Streusel Topping: In a medium bowl combine 3/4 cup flour, 1/2 teaspoon cinnamon, brown sugar, oats, and lemon peel. Mix thoroughly, then cut in 1/2 cup butter or margarine until mixture is crumbly. Remove filling from oven and sprinkle streusel on top.

Step 6

Reduce heat to 375 degrees F (190 degrees C). Bake an additional 30 to 35 minutes, until streusel is browned and apples are tender. Cover loosely with aluminum foil to prevent excess browning.

Nutrition Facts

Per Serving:

440.8 calories; protein 3.5g 7% DV; carbohydrates 63.4g 21% DV; fat 20.4g 31% DV; cholesterol 38.1mg 13% DV; sodium 209.8mg 8% DV.

Top Sirloin Roast

Prep: 30 mins **Cook:** 1 hr **Additional:** 15 mins **Total:** 1 hr 45 mins **Servings:** 8 **Yield:** 8 servings

Ingredients

- 1 (3 pound) beef top-sirloin roast
- 3 cloves garlic, slivered, or to taste
- 3 cloves garlic, minced
- 1 teaspoon ground paprika, or to taste
- 1 teaspoon salt, or to taste
- 1 teaspoon freshly ground black pepper, or to taste
- 6 eaches Yukon Gold potatoes, quartered
- 5 carrot, (7-1/2")s carrots, cut into 2-inch pieces
- 2 large sweet onions, quartered
- 3 cubes beef bouillon
- ½ cup hot water
- 1 cup beef broth
- ½ cup beer
- 2 leaf (blank)s bay leaves, broken, or more to taste
- 2 large red bell peppers, cut into 2-inch pieces
- ½ cup mushrooms

Directions

Step 1

Make small slits in the roast using a sharp knife; tuck slivered garlic into each slit. Rub minced garlic, paprika, salt, and ground black pepper over the entire roast. Set aside until roast comes to room temperature, 15 to 30 minutes.

Step 2

Preheat oven to 325 degrees F (165 degrees C).

Step 3

Arrange potatoes, carrots, and onions in an even layer in a 9x12-inch roasting pan. Dissolve beef bouillon cubes in hot water in a small bowl and pour over vegetables. Pour in beef broth and beer.

Step 4

Place roast on top of the vegetables, making sure it is not submerged in the broth mixture. Place bay leaf pieces around the roast.

Step 5

Bake roast in the preheated oven until internal temperature reaches 150 degrees F (66 degrees C) for medium, 45 to 60 minutes. Transfer roast to a platter; cover with aluminum foil, and allow to rest until internal temperature reaches 155 degrees (68 degrees C), about 10 minutes.

Step 6

Increase oven temperature to 425 degrees F (220 degrees C). Add red pepper and mushrooms to the roasting pan and return it to the oven. Bake until vegetables are tender and lightly browned, 15 to 20 minutes.

Step 7

Thinly slice the roast crosswise. Serve with vegetables; spoon pan juices over meat and vegetables.

Cook's Notes:

Leave the skin on the potatoes if desired.

Substitute green bell pepper for the red if preferred.

You may prefer to cook the roast separately from the vegetables.

Nutrition Facts

Per Serving:

400.5 calories; protein 35.1g 70% DV; carbohydrates 40.3g 13% DV; fat 10.4g 16% DV; cholesterol 73.7mg 25% DV; sodium 820.6mg 33% DV.

Pumpkin Crunch Cake

Prep: 15 mins **Cook:** 1 hr **Total:** 1 hr 15 mins **Servings:** 18 **Yield:** 1 - 9x13 inch cake

Ingredients

- 1 (15 ounce) can pumpkin puree
- 1 (12 fluid ounce) can evaporated milk
- 4 large eggs eggs
- 1 ½ cups white sugar
- 2 teaspoons pumpkin pie spice
- 1 teaspoon salt
- 1 (18.25 ounce) package yellow cake mix
- 1 cup chopped pecans
- 1 cup margarine, melted
- 1 (8 ounce) container frozen whipped topping, thawed

Directions

Step 1

Preheat oven to 350 degrees F (175 degrees C). Lightly grease one 9x13 inch baking pan.

Step 2

In a large bowl, combine pumpkin, evaporated milk, eggs, sugar, pumpkin pie spice, and salt. Mix well, and spread into the prepared pan.

Step 3

Sprinkle cake mix over the top of the pumpkin mixture, and pat down. Sprinkle chopped pecans evenly over the cake mix, then drizzle with melted margarine.

Step 4

Bake for 60 to 80 minutes, or until done. Top with whipped topping when ready to serve.

Nutrition Facts

Per Serving:

411.8 calories; protein 5.2g 10% DV; carbohydrates 47.2g 15% DV; fat 23.6g 36% DV; cholesterol 48mg 16% DV; sodium 532.8mg 21% DV.

Caramel Apple Pork Chops

Prep: 20 mins **Cook:** 25 mins **Total:** 45 mins **Servings:** 4 **Yield:** 4 servings

Ingredients

- 4 raw chop with refuse, 106 g; yields excluding refuses (3/4 inch) thick pork chops
- 1 teaspoon vegetable oil
- 2 tablespoons brown sugar
- 1 pinch salt and pepper to taste
- ⅛ teaspoon ground cinnamon
- ⅛ teaspoon ground nutmeg
- 2 tablespoons unsalted butter
- 2 medium (2-3/4" dia) (approx 3 per lb)s tart apples - peeled, cored and sliced
- 3 tablespoons pecans

Directions

Step 1

Preheat oven to 175 degrees F (80 degrees C). Place a medium dish in the oven to warm.

Step 2

Heat a large skillet over medium-high heat. Brush chops lightly with oil and place in hot pan. Cook for 5 to 6 minutes, turning occasionally, or until done. Transfer to the warm dish, and keep warm in the preheated oven.

Step 3

In a small bowl, combine brown sugar, salt and pepper, cinnamon and nutmeg. Add butter to skillet, and stir in brown sugar mixture and apples. Cover and cook until apples are just tender. Remove apples with a slotted spoon and arrange on top of chops. Keep warm in the preheated oven.

Step 4

Continue cooking sauce uncovered in skillet, until thickened slightly. Spoon sauce over apples and chops. Sprinkle with pecans.

Nutrition Facts

Per Serving:

262.2 calories; protein 13.8g 28% DV; carbohydrates 17.1g 6% DV; fat 16g 25% DV; cholesterol 47.6mg 16% DV; sodium 27.4mg 1% DV.

Apple Cake IV

Servings: 24 **Yield:** 1 - 9x13 inch pan

Ingredients

- 5 medium (2-3/4" dia) (approx 3 per lb)s apple - peeled, cored and sliced
- 2 cups all-purpose flour
- ½ teaspoon salt
- 4 teaspoons ground cinnamon
- 4 teaspoons baking powder
- 4 large eggs eggs
- 2 cups white sugar
- 1 cup vegetable oil
- 2 teaspoons vanilla extract
- 1 cup chopped walnuts
- 4 teaspoons white sugar
- 1 teaspoon ground cinnamon

Directions

Step 1

Preheat oven to 350 degrees F (175 degrees C) lightly grease and flour a 9x13 inch pan.

Step 2

Sift together flour, salt, cinnamon and baking powder. Set aside.

Step 3

In a large bowl, beat eggs and sugar for 15 minutes on high speed with an electric mixer. Add oil and blend in.

Step 4

Add four mixture and mix well. Add vanilla. Fold in apples and nuts. Pour batter into 9x13 inch pan.

Step 5

In a small bowl, mix 4 teaspoons sugar with 1 teaspoon cinnamon. Sprinkle over cake.

Step 6

Bake at 350 degrees F (175 degrees C) for 50 to 60 minutes or until a toothpick inserted into center of cake comes out clean.

Nutrition Facts

Per Serving:

247.5 calories; protein 3g 6% DV; carbohydrates 30.7g 10% DV; fat 13.3g 21% DV; cholesterol 31mg 10% DV; sodium 142.1mg 6% DV.

Better Baked Beans

Prep: 10 mins **Cook:** 35 mins **Total:** 45 mins **Servings:** 12 **Yield:** 12 servings

Ingredients

- 2 (28 ounce) cans baked beans
- 1 small onion, chopped
- 2 tablespoons brown sugar
- 3 tablespoons pancake syrup
- 2 tablespoons ketchup
- 2 teaspoons prepared yellow mustard
- 4 slices bacon

Directions

Step 1

Preheat the oven to 350 degrees F (175 degrees C).

Step 2

In a large bowl, stir together the baked beans, onion, brown sugar, syrup, ketchup and mustard. Pour into a 9x13 inch baking dish, and lay strips of bacon across the top.

Step 3

Bake for 35 to 40 minutes in the preheated oven, until the bacon is browned and the beans have thickened.

Nutrition Facts

Per Serving:

192.2 calories; protein 7.4g 15% DV; carbohydrates 34.6g 11% DV; fat 4.7g 7% DV; cholesterol 6.3mg 2% DV; sodium 557.7mg 22% DV.

Pumpkin Spice Cookie

Prep: 15 mins **Cook:** 20 mins **Total:** 35 mins **Servings:** 24 **Yield:** 2 dozen cookies

Ingredients

- 1 (18.25 ounce) package spice cake mix
- 1 (15 ounce) can solid pack pumpkin

Directions

Step 1

Preheat oven to 350 degrees F (175 degrees C). Grease cookie sheets.

Step 2

In a large bowl, stir together the cake mix and pumpkin until well blended. Drop by rounded spoonfuls onto the prepared cookie sheet.

Step 3

Bake for 18 to 20 minutes in the preheated oven. Allow cookies to cool on baking sheet for 5 minutes before removing to a wire rack to cool completely.

Nutrition Facts

Per Serving:

98 calories; protein 1.5g 3% DV; carbohydrates 17.2g 6% DV; fat 2.7g 4% DV; cholesterolmg; sodium 187.8mg 8% DV.

Chef John's Beef Goulash

Prep: 30 mins **Cook:** 2 hrs **Total:** 2 hrs 30 mins **Servings:** 4 **Yield:** 4 servings

Ingredients

- 2 ½ pounds boneless beef chuck roast, cut into 2-inch cubes
- 1 pinch salt and ground black pepper to taste
- 2 tablespoons vegetable oil
- 2 medium (2-1/2" dia)s onions, chopped
- 2 teaspoons olive oil
- ½ teaspoon salt
- 2 tablespoons Hungarian paprika
- 2 teaspoons caraway seeds, crushed
- 1 teaspoon freshly ground black pepper
- 1 teaspoon dried marjoram
- ½ teaspoon ground thyme
- ½ teaspoon cayenne pepper
- 4 cups chicken broth, divided
- ¼ cup tomato paste
- 3 cloves garlic, crushed
- 2 tablespoons balsamic vinegar
- 1 teaspoon white sugar
- ½ teaspoon salt, or to taste
- 1 bay leaf

Directions

Step 1

Season beef with salt and black pepper. Heat vegetable oil in a large skillet over high heat; cook and stir beef in hot oil in batches until browned on all sides, about 5 minutes per batch. Transfer to a large stockpot and reserve drippings in the skillet.

Step 2

Return skillet to medium heat; stir onions into the reserved drippings, drizzle olive oil over onions, season with 1/2 teaspoon salt and cook until onion has softened, about 5 minutes. Transfer to the stockpot with beef.

Step 3

Combine paprika, caraway seeds, black pepper, marjoram, thyme, and cayenne pepper in the skillet and toast over medium heat until fragrant, about 3 minutes. Add 1 cup chicken broth and stir; transfer to the beef and onion mixture.

Step 4

Stir 3 cups chicken broth into beef mixture. Add tomato paste, garlic, vinegar, sugar, 1/2 teaspoon salt, and bay leaf; place stockpot over high heat and bring to a boil. Reduce heat to low and simmer until a fork inserts easily into the meat, 1 1/2 to 2 hours.

Chef's Note:

Real goulash is more like a soup, so if you want yours thinner, just add 2 or 3 extra cups of broth.

Nutrition Facts

Per Serving:

573.3 calories; protein 36g 72% DV; carbohydrates 13.4g 4% DV; fat 41.2g 63% DV; cholesterol 134mg 45% DV; sodium 1756.6mg 70% DV.

Vegetarian Moussaka

Prep: 30 mins **Cook:** 1 hr 30 mins **Total:** 2 hrs **Servings:** 7 **Yield:** 8 to 10 servings

Ingredients

- 1 eggplant, thinly sliced
- 1 tablespoon olive oil, or more as needed
- 1 large zucchini, thinly sliced
- 2 medium (2-1/4" to 3" dia, raw)s potatoes, thinly sliced
- 1 onion, sliced
- 1 clove garlic, chopped
- 1 tablespoon white vinegar
- 1 (14.5 ounce) can whole peeled tomatoes, chopped
- ½ (14.5 ounce) can lentils, drained with liquid reserved
- 1 teaspoon dried oregano

- 2 tablespoons chopped fresh parsley
- salt and ground black pepper to taste
- 1 cup crumbled feta cheese
- 1 ½ tablespoons butter
- 2 tablespoons all-purpose flour
- 1 ¼ cups milk
- 1 pinch ground black pepper to taste
- 1 pinch ground nutmeg
- 1 egg, beaten
- ¼ cup grated Parmesan cheese

Directions

Step 1

Sprinkle eggplant slices with salt and set aside for 30 minutes. Rinse and pat dry.

Step 2

Preheat oven to 375 degrees F (190 degrees C).

Step 3

Heat oil in a large skillet over medium-high heat. Rinse and pat eggplant dry. Cook eggplant and zucchini in hot oil until lightly browned on both sides, about 3 minutes per side; remove with a slotted spoon to drain on a paper towel-lined plate, reserving as much oil as possible in the skillet

Step 4

Adding more oil to skillet as needed and let it get hot. Cook potato slices in hot oil until browned, 3 to 5 minutes per side; remove with slotted spoon and drain on a paper towel-lined plate, again reserving oil in the skillet.

Step 5

Saute onion and garlic in reserved oil until lightly browned, 5 to 7 minutes. Pour in vinegar, bring to a boil, and reduce heat to medium-low; cook until liquid is reduced in volume and thick. Stir in tomatoes, lentils, 1/2 the juice from lentils, oregano and parsley. Cover, reduce heat to medium-low, and simmer 15 minutes.

Step 6

Layer about 1/3 of the eggplant, 1/3 of the zucchini, 1/2 the potatoes, 1/2 the onions, and 1/2 the feta into a 13x9-inch baking dish. Pour tomato mixture over vegetables; repeat layering, finishing with a layer of eggplant and zucchini.

Step 7

Cover and bake in preheated oven for 25 minutes.

Step 8

Stir butter, flour, and milk together in a small saucepan; bring to a slow boil, whisking constantly until thick and smooth. Season with pepper and nutmeg; stir. Remove from heat, cool for 5 minutes, and stir in beaten egg.

Step 9

Pour sauce over vegetables and sprinkle with Parmesan cheese. Bake, uncovered, for another 25 to 30 minutes.

Nutrition Facts

Per Serving:

239.8 calories; protein 10.2g 20% DV; carbohydrates 25.5g 8% DV; fat 11.8g 18% DV; cholesterol 58.2mg 19% DV; sodium 425.7mg 17% DV.

Pure Maple Candy

Prep: 1 min **Cook:** 10 mins **Additional:** 40 mins **Total:** 51 mins **Servings:** 18 **Yield:** 18 maple leaves

Ingredients

- 2 cups pure maple syrup
- ½ cup chopped walnuts

Directions

Step 1

In a large heavy-bottomed saucepan, bring the maple syrup to a boil over medium-high heat stirring occasionally. Boil until syrup reaches 235 degrees F (110 degrees C) on a candy thermometer.

Step 2

Remove from heat and cool to 175 degrees F (80 degrees C) without stirring, about 10 minutes.

Step 3

Stir mixture rapidly with a wooden spoon for about 5 minutes until the color turns lighter and mixture becomes thick and creamy. Stir in chopped nuts, if desired.

Step 4

Pour into molds. Set aside to cool. Once cool, unmold candy. Store in airtight containers up to 1 month.

Nutrition Facts

Per Serving:

113.2 calories; protein 0.5g 1% DV; carbohydrates 23.9g 8% DV; fat 2.2g 4% DV; cholesterolmg; sodium 3.2mg.

Cosmo-Style Pomegranate Martini

Ingredients

- 2 fluid ounces citron vodka
- 1 fluid ounce Cointreau or other orange liqueur
- 2 fluid ounces pomegranate juice
- ½ fluid ounce lemon juice

Directions

Step 1

Pour the vodka, Cointreau, pomegranate juice, and lemon juice into a cocktail shaker over ice. Cover, and shake until the outside of the shaker has frosted. Strain into a chilled martini glass to serve.

Nutrition Facts

Per Serving:

345.4 calories; protein 0.1g; carbohydrates 45.2g 15% DV; fat 0.1g; cholesterolmg; sodium 2.5mg.

Apple Pie in a Jar Drink

Prep: 5 mins **Cook:** 15 mins **Additional:** 4 hrs **Total:** 4 hrs 20 mins **Servings:** 80 **Yield:** 5 quarts

Ingredients

- 1 gallon apple cider
- 1 gallon apple juice
- 6 (3 inch) cinnamon sticks
- 1 ½ cups white sugar, or to taste
- 1 (1 liter) bottle 190 proof grain alcohol (such as Everclear™)

Directions

Step 1

Place the apple cider, apple juice, cinnamon sticks, and sugar into a large pot. Bring to a boil over medium-high heat, stirring until the sugar has dissolved. Remove from the heat, and discard the cinnamon sticks. Allow the mixture to cool to room temperature, then stir in the grain alcohol. Pour into quart-size canning jars, seal with the lids and rings, and refrigerate until ready to serve.

Cook's Note:

You can store this in the refrigerator for at least 6 months. I've heard of people storing it for a year or more.

Nutrition Facts

Per Serving:

99.5 calories; proteing; carbohydrates 16.4g 5% DV; fat 0.1g; cholesterolmg; sodium 7.1mg.

Classic Cherries Jubilee

Prep: 10 mins Cook: 20 mins Total: 30 mins Servings: 6 Yield: 6 servings

Ingredients

- ½ cup white sugar
- 2 tablespoons cornstarch
- ¼ cup cold water
- ¼ cup orange juice
- 1 pound Bing or other dark, sweet cherries, rinsed and pitted (or use frozen pitted cherries)
- ½ teaspoon finely grated orange zest
- ¼ teaspoon cherry extract
- ¼ cup brandy
- 3 cups vanilla bean ice cream

Directions

Step 1

Whisk together the sugar and cornstarch in a wide saucepan. Stir in the water and orange juice; bring to a boil over medium-high heat, whisking until thickened. Stir in the cherries and orange zest, return to a boil, then reduce heat, and simmer for 10 minutes. While the cherries are cooking, spoon the ice cream into serving bowls.

Step 2

Remove the cherries from the heat, and stir in the cherry extract. Pour in the brandy, and ignite with a long lighter. Gently shake the pan until the blue flame has extinguished itself. Spoon the cherries over the bowls of ice cream.

Note on flambeing

The flames may get quite high when flambeing, so pay attention to anything flammable above and around where you ignite the cherries. When the initial large flame has died down, a small blue flame will continue to burn for several seconds. Shake or stir the cherries gently to expose more alcohol to the flame, being careful that they do not burn. The goal is to have the small, blue flame burn for as long as possible, thereby reducing the raw alcohol flavor, caramelizing the sugars, and entertaining your guests!

Nutrition Facts

Per Serving:

295.7 calories; protein 3.3g 7% DV; carbohydrates 48.3g 16% DV; fat 8g 12% DV; cholesterol 29mg 10% DV; sodium 53.5mg 2% DV.

Hot Crab Dip

Prep: 10 mins Cook: 30 mins Total: 40 mins Servings: 40 Yield: 5 cups

Ingredients

- 2 (8 ounce) packages cream cheese, softened
- 4 tablespoons mayonnaise

- 2 cups shredded Cheddar cheese
- 2 (6 ounce) cans crabmeat
- 1 ½ tablespoons fresh lemon juice
- 2 teaspoons hot sauce
- 2 tablespoons Worcestershire sauce
- paprika, for garnish

Directions

Step 1

Preheat oven to 350 degrees F (175 degrees C).

Step 2

In a medium bowl, mix the cream cheese, mayonnaise, Cheddar cheese, crabmeat, lemon juice, hot sauce and Worcestershire sauce. Transfer to a shallow 9x13 inch baking dish. Garnish with paprika.

Step 3

Bake in the preheated oven 30 minutes, or until golden brown and bubbly.

Nutrition Facts

Per Serving:

80.9 calories; protein 4g 8% DV; carbohydrates 0.6g; fat 7g 11% DV; cholesterol 26.3mg 9% DV; sodium 118.5mg 5% DV.

White Chocolate and Cranberry Cookies

Prep: 15 mins **Cook:** 10 mins **Additional:** 25 mins **Total:** 50 mins **Servings:** 24 **Yield:** 2 dozen

Ingredients

- ½ cup butter, softened
- ½ cup packed brown sugar
- ½ cup white sugar
- 1 egg
- 1 tablespoon brandy
- 1 ½ cups all-purpose flour
- ½ teaspoon baking soda
- ¾ cup white chocolate chips
- 1 cup dried cranberries

Directions

Step 1

Preheat oven to 375 degrees F (190 degrees C). Grease cookie sheets.

Step 2

In a large bowl, cream together the butter, brown sugar, and white sugar until smooth. Beat in the egg and brandy. Combine the flour and baking soda; stir into the sugar mixture. Mix in the white chocolate chips and cranberries. Drop by heaping spoonfuls onto prepared cookie sheets.

Step 3

Bake for 8 to 10 minutes in the preheated oven. For best results, take them out while they are still doughy. Allow cookies to cool for 1 minute on the cookie sheets before transferring to wire racks to cool completely.

Nutrition Facts

Per Serving:

147.4 calories; protein 1.5g 3% DV; carbohydrates 21.9g 7% DV; fat 6.1g 9% DV; cholesterol 19.1mg 6% DV; sodium 63.8mg 3% DV.

Apple Pie Spice Mix

Prep: 5 mins **Total:** 5 mins **Servings:** 2 **Yield:** 2 tablespoons

Ingredients

- 4 teaspoons ground cinnamon
- 2 teaspoons ground nutmeg
- 1 teaspoon ground cardamom

Directions

Step 1

In a small bowl, combine cinnamon, nutmeg and cardamom. Store in a sealed jar.

Nutrition Facts

Per Serving:

30.2 calories; protein 0.5g 1% DV; carbohydrates 5.9g 2% DV; fat 1.2g 2% DV; cholesterolmg; sodium 1.1mg.

Candied Apples II

Prep: 10 mins **Cook:** 30 mins **Total:** 40 mins **Servings:** 15 **Yield:** 15 candied apples

Ingredients

- 15 medium (2-3/4" dia) (approx 3 per lb)s apples
- 2 cups white sugar
- 1 cup light corn syrup
- 1 ½ cups water
- 8 drops red food coloring

Directions

Step 1

Lightly grease cookie sheets. Insert craft sticks into whole, stemmed apples.

Step 2

In a medium saucepan over medium-high heat, combine sugar, corn syrup and water. Heat to 300 to 310 degrees F (149 to 154 degrees C), or until a small amount of syrup dropped into cold water forms hard, brittle threads. Remove from heat and stir in food coloring.

Step 3

Holding apple by its stick, dip in syrup and remove and turn to coat evenly. Place on prepared sheets to harden.

Nutrition Facts

Per Serving:

236.8 calories; protein 0.4g 1% DV; carbohydrates 62.5g 20% DV; fat 0.2g; cholesterolmg; sodium 15mg 1% DV.

Millionaire Pie

Servings: 16 **Yield:** 2 pies

Ingredients

- 1 (8 ounce) package cream cheese, softened
- 1 (14 ounce) can sweetened condensed milk
- 1 (12 ounce) container frozen whipped topping, thawed
- 1 (20 ounce) can crushed pineapple, drained
- 1 ½ cups chopped pecans
- 2 (9 inch) prepared graham cracker crusts

Directions

Step 1

Blend together the cream cheese and condensed milk; gently fold in the whipped topping.

Step 2

Stir in the crushed pineapple and pecans; pour into pie crusts and refrigerate for 3 to 4 hours.

Nutrition Facts

Per Serving:

433.5 calories; protein 5.6g 11% DV; carbohydrates 44.9g 15% DV; fat 27.1g 42% DV; cholesterol 23.7mg 8% DV; sodium 248.7mg 10% DV.

Pear or Apple Cobbler

Prep: 15 mins **Cook:** 45 mins **Total:** 1 hr **Servings:** 9 **Yield:** 9 servings

Ingredients

- 4 eaches pears, cored and cut into 1/2-inch slices
- 1 teaspoon lemon juice
- ⅓ cup maple syrup
- 2 tablespoons melted butter
- Topping:
- 1 cup rolled oats
- 1 cup brown sugar
- ½ cup melted butter
- ½ cup all-purpose flour
- 1 teaspoon ground cinnamon

Directions

Step 1

Preheat oven to 375 degrees F (190 degrees C).

Step 2

Toss pears and lemon juice together in a bowl until coated; spread into a 9x9-inch baking dish. Pour maple syrup and 2 tablespoons melted butter over pear mixture; toss to coat.

Step 3

Mix oats, brown sugar, 1/2 cup melted butter, flour, and cinnamon together in a bowl until crumbly; sprinkle over pear mixture.

Step 4

Bake in the preheated oven until crust is golden and pears are tender, about 45 minutes.

Cook's Note:

Granny Smith apples work well in place of pears.

Nutrition Facts

Per Serving:

339.3 calories; protein 2.4g 5% DV; carbohydrates 54.9g 18% DV; fat 13.6g 21% DV; cholesterol 33.9mg 11% DV; sodium 100.2mg 4% DV.

Easy Apple Coffee Cake

Prep: 30 mins **Cook:** 1 hr **Additional:** 30 mins **Total:** 2 hrs **Servings:** 12 **Yield:** 1 10-inch Bundt pan

Ingredients

- 1 (18.25 ounce) package yellow cake mix
- 1 (3.4 ounce) package instant vanilla pudding mix
- 4 large eggs eggs
- 1 cup sour cream

- ½ cup vegetable oil
- 6 medium (2-3/4" dia) (approx 3 per lb)s apples - peeled, cored and sliced
- ½ cup white sugar
- 2 teaspoons ground cinnamon
- ½ cup chopped walnuts

Directions

Step 1

Preheat oven to 350 degrees F (175 degrees C). Grease and flour a 10 inch Bundt pan.

Step 2

In a large bowl, stir together the cake mix and instant pudding mix. Add the eggs, sour cream and oil, mix until well blended. In a small bowl combine the sugar, cinnamon and walnuts.

Step 3

Pour half of the batter into the prepared pan, then place a layer of sliced apples over the batter and sprinkle with half of the cinnamon walnut mixture. Pour the remaining batter over the top and repeat with the remaining apples and cinnamon walnut mixture.

Step 4

Bake for 60 to 70 minutes in the preheated oven. Cool for 1/2 hour before removing from pan to cool completely.

Nutrition Facts

Per Serving:

456.9 calories; protein 5.5g 11% DV; carbohydrates 59.4g 19% DV; fat 23.2g 36% DV; cholesterol 71.3mg 24% DV; sodium 430.8mg 17% DV.

Apple Crisp IV

Servings: 18 **Yield:** 1 - 9x13 inch pan

Ingredients

- 2 cups all-purpose flour
- 2 cups rolled oats
- 1 teaspoon ground cinnamon
- ½ teaspoon ground nutmeg
- 1 ½ cups packed brown sugar
- 1 ½ cups butter
- 2 quarts peeled, cored and sliced apples

Directions

Step 1

Preheat oven to 350 degrees F (175 degrees C).

Step 2

In a large bowl, combine the flour, oatmeal, cinnamon, nutmeg and brown sugar. Cut butter into mixture until crumbly.

Step 3

Take half of the mixture and pat it into the bottom of a 9x13 inch baking dish.

Step 4

Cover crumb mixture with apple slices, then sprinkle apple slices with remaining crumb mixture.

Step 5

Bake at 350 degrees F (175 degrees C) for 45 to 50 minutes or until apples are tender.

Nutrition Facts

Per Serving:

319.4 calories; protein 3g 6% DV; carbohydrates 42.5g 14% DV; fat 16.2g 25% DV; cholesterol 40.7mg 14% DV; sodium 115.5mg 5% DV.

Squash Relish

Prep: 30 mins **Cook:** 25 mins **Additional:** 2 hrs **Total:** 2 hrs 55 mins **Servings:** 192 **Yield:** 6 pints

Ingredients

- 8 cups diced yellow squash
- 2 cups diced onion
- 2 eaches red bell peppers, diced
- 2 eaches green bell peppers, diced
- 3 tablespoons salt
- 3 cups white sugar
- 2 cups vinegar
- 2 teaspoons celery seeds
- 2 teaspoons whole mustard seeds
- 6 eaches (1 pint) canning jars with lids and rings

Directions

Step 1

Place the squash, onion, and red and green bell peppers into a large bowl, and sprinkle with salt. Toss to combine, and allow the vegetables to drain for 1 hour. Discard juice.

Step 2

Place the sugar, vinegar, celery seeds, and mustard seeds into a large pot, and bring to a boil over medium heat, stirring to dissolve sugar. Stir in the squash mixture, and return to a boil. Cook the mixture until the vegetables are tender, about 15 minutes.

Step 3

Sterilize the jars and lids in boiling water for at least 5 minutes. Pack the squash relish into the hot, sterilized jars, filling the jars to within 1/4 inch of the top. Run a knife or a thin spatula around the insides of the jars after they have been filled to remove any air bubbles. Wipe the rims of the jars with a moist paper towel to remove any food residue. Top with lids, and screw on rings.

Step 4

Place a rack in the bottom of a large stockpot and fill halfway with water. Bring to a boil over high heat, then carefully lower the jars into the pot using a holder. Leave a 2-inch space between the jars. Pour in more boiling water if necessary until the water level is at least 1 inch above the tops of the jars. Bring the water to a full boil, cover the pot, and process for 10 minutes, or the time recommended for your area.

Step 5

Remove the jars from the pot, and place onto a cloth-covered or wood surface, several inches apart, until cool. Once cool, press the top of each lid with a finger, ensuring that the seal is tight (lid does not move up or down at all). Store in the refrigerator.

Nutrition Facts
Per Serving:
14.7 calories; protein 0.1g; carbohydrates 3.7g 1% DV; fatg; cholesterolmg; sodium 109.3mg 4% DV.

Aunt Carol's Apple Pie

Prep: 30 mins **Cook:** 1 hr **Total:** 1 hr 30 mins **Servings:** 8 **Yield:** 1 10-inch pie

Ingredients

- 2 pounds Granny Smith apples
- 1 cup white sugar
- ½ cup brown sugar
- 2 teaspoons ground cinnamon
- ½ cup all-purpose flour
- 2 tablespoons butter
- 1 tablespoon white sugar
- 1 recipe pastry for a 9 inch double crust pie

Directions

Step 1

Peel and slice apples. Toss with sugars, cinnamon and flour. Set aside.

Step 2

Roll crust to make slightly larger to fit 10-inch glass pie pan. Fit bottom crust in pie pan. Turn in apple mixture and dot with butter. Put crust on top and crimp edges of crust together.

Step 3

Preheat oven to 450 degrees F (230 degrees C).

Step 4

Wet hands with water and dampen top of pie. Sprinkle with additional sugar. Puncture top of pie with fork so the steam can escape.

Step 5

Bake for 15 minutes in preheated oven. Reduce heat to 350 degrees F (175 degrees C) and continue baking for about 45 minutes more, until crust is golden brown. It's a good practice to place a piece of aluminum foil slightly larger than the pie under the pie plate to catch overflows. Serve warm.

Nutrition Facts

Per Serving:

492 calories; protein 3.9g 8% DV; carbohydrates 81g 26% DV; fat 18.3g 28% DV; cholesterol 7.6mg 3% DV; sodium 257mg 10% DV.

Vegetarian Gravy

Prep: 10 mins **Cook:** 20 mins **Total:** 30 mins **Servings:** 10 **Yield:** 2 1/2 cups

Ingredients

- ½ cup vegetable oil
- ⅓ cup chopped onion
- 5 cloves garlic, minced
- ½ cup all-purpose flour
- 4 teaspoons nutritional yeast
- 4 tablespoons light soy sauce
- 2 cups vegetable broth
- ½ teaspoon dried sage
- ½ teaspoon salt
- ¼ teaspoon ground black pepper

Directions

Step 1

Heat oil in a medium saucepan over medium heat. Saute onion and garlic until soft and translucent, about 5 minutes. Stir in flour, nutritional yeast, and soy sauce to form a smooth paste. Gradually whisk in the broth.

Season with sage, salt, and pepper. Bring to a boil. Reduce heat, and simmer, stirring constantly, for 8 to 10 minutes, or until thickened.

Nutrition Facts
Per Serving:

133.5 calories; protein 1.7g 4% DV; carbohydrates 6.9g 2% DV; fat 11.2g 17% DV; cholesterolmg; sodium 381.8mg 15% DV.

Pumpkin Pie Squares

Servings: 24 **Yield:** 1 9x13 pan

Ingredients

- 1 cup all-purpose flour
- ½ cup rolled oats
- ½ cup packed brown sugar
- ½ cup butter
- 2 cups pumpkin puree
- 1 (12 fluid ounce) can evaporated milk
- 2 large egg whites egg whites
- ¾ cup white sugar
- ½ teaspoon salt
- 1 teaspoon ground cinnamon
- ½ teaspoon ground ginger
- ½ teaspoon ground cloves
- ½ cup chopped walnuts
- ½ cup packed brown sugar
- 2 tablespoons butter
- 1 cup whipped cream

Directions

Step 1

Preheat oven to 350 degrees F (175 degrees C). Spray or grease one 9x13 inch pan.

Step 2

Mix together the flour, oatmeal, brown sugar and butter or margarine. Press into pan; bake for 20 minutes or until golden brown.

Step 3

In a large deep metal bowl, beat egg whites until soft peaks form.

Step 4

Blend together the pumpkin, evaporated milk, egg whites, sugar, salt, cinnamon, ginger and clove. Pour custard into baked crust; bake for 30 minutes or until firm.

Step 5

Mix together the chopped nuts, brown sugar and butter. Sprinkle topping on custard and bake additional 15 minutes. Remove from oven and allow to cool. Cut into squares and top with whipped cream if desired.

Nutrition Facts

Per Serving:

176.2 calories; protein 2.8g 6% DV; carbohydrates 23.7g 8% DV; fat 8.3g 13% DV; cholesterol 19.2mg 6% DV; sodium 110.2mg 4% DV.

Quick Apple Pie Bread

Prep: 20 mins **Cook:** 1 hr **Additional:** 15 mins **Total:** 1 hr 35 mins **Servings:** 10 **Yield:** 1 loaf

Ingredients

- 1 (21 ounce) can apple filling
- 1 cup butter, at room temperature
- ½ cup white sugar
- ½ cup (packed) dark brown sugar
- 2 large eggs eggs
- 1 tablespoon vanilla extract
- 2 cups all-purpose flour
- 1 teaspoon baking soda
- 1 teaspoon ground cinnamon
- ½ teaspoon salt
- ¾ cup raisins
- ¾ cup chopped walnuts

Directions

Step 1

Preheat oven to 350 degrees F (175 degrees C). Lightly grease a 9x5 loaf pan.

Step 2

In a medium bowl, use a potato masher to break up apples in the filling; set aside. In a large mixing bowl, cream together butter, white sugar, and brown sugar. Stir in eggs, apples, and vanilla extract until well blended. Sift together flour, baking soda, cinnamon, and salt. Stir into apple mixture, then stir in raisins and walnuts. Pour batter into prepared pan.

Step 3

Bake in preheated oven for 60 minute, until a toothpick inserted into center of the loaf comes out clean. Let bread cool in pan for 15 minutes, then turn out onto a wire rack to cool completely.

Nutrition Facts

Per Serving:

508.8 calories; protein 5.9g 12% DV; carbohydrates 66.9g 22% DV; fat 25.6g 39% DV; cholesterol 86mg 29% DV; sodium 418.3mg 17% DV.

Mom's Applesauce Pancakes

Prep: 10 mins **Cook:** 20 mins **Total:** 30 mins **Servings:** 4 **Yield:** 4 servings

Ingredients

- 2 cups dry pancake mix
- 1 teaspoon ground cinnamon
- 2 large eggs eggs
- 1 cup applesauce
- 1 teaspoon lemon juice
- ½ cup milk

Directions

Step 1

In a large bowl, stir together pancake mix and cinnamon. Make a well in the center of the pancake mix. Add the eggs, applesauce, lemon juice and milk; stir until smooth.

Step 2

Heat a lightly oiled griddle or frying pan over medium high heat. Pour or scoop the batter onto the griddle, using approximately 1/4 cup for each pancake. Brown on both sides and serve hot.

Nutrition Facts

Per Serving:

319.3 calories; protein 10.1g 20% DV; carbohydrates 60.2g 19% DV; fat 4.3g 7% DV; cholesterol 95.4mg 32% DV; sodium 1016.1mg 41% DV.

Autumn Spiced Butternut Squash Bread

Prep: 15 mins **Cook:** 1 hr **Additional:** 1 hr **Total:** 2 hrs 15 mins **Servings:** 20 **Yield:** 2 9x5-inch loaves

Ingredients

- 2 ⅔ cups white sugar
- ⅔ cup shortening
- 2 cups pureed cooked butternut squash
- 4 large eggs eggs

- ⅔ cup water
- 3 ⅓ cups all-purpose flour
- 2 teaspoons baking soda
- 2 teaspoons baking powder
- 1 ½ teaspoons salt
- 1 teaspoon ground cinnamon
- 1 teaspoon ground cloves
- ⅔ cup chopped walnuts
- ⅔ cup raisins

Directions

Step 1

Preheat oven to 350 degrees F (175 degrees C). Grease two 9x5-inch loaf pans.

Step 2

Beat sugar and shortening together in a bowl until fluffy. Stir butternut squash, eggs, and water into sugar mixture.

Step 3

Mix flour, baking soda, baking powder, salt, cinnamon, and cloves in another bowl; stir into sugar mixture. Add nuts and raisins; stir until batter is just blended. Pour batter into prepared loaf pans.

Step 4

Bake in the preheated oven until a toothpick inserted into the center comes out clean, about 1 hour. Cool in the pans for 15 minutes before removing to cool completely on a wire rack.

Nutrition Facts

Per Serving:

305.9 calories; protein 4.5g 9% DV; carbohydrates 50.2g 16% DV; fat 10.6g 16% DV; cholesterol 37.2mg 12% DV; sodium 365.1mg 15% DV.

Apple Dumplings I

Prep: 20 mins **Cook:** 35 mins **Total:** 55 mins **Servings:** 8 **Yield:** 8 dumplings

Ingredients

- 1 (16 ounce) can refrigerated flaky biscuit dough
- 4 small (2-1/2" dia) (approx 4 per lb)s apples - peeled, cored and halved
- 1 cup white sugar
- 1 cup water
- ½ cup butter, melted
- 2 teaspoons vanilla extract
- ½ teaspoon ground cinnamon

Directions

Step 1

Preheat oven to 350 degrees F (175 degrees C).

Step 2

Butter a 7x11 inch baking pan. Separate biscuit dough into 8 pieces. Flatten each piece of dough into a circle. Wrap one biscuit around each apple half and place, seam side down, in pan.

Step 3

In small bowl, combine sugar, water, melted butter and vanilla. Pour mixture over dumplings in pan. Sprinkle cinnamon on top. Bake 35 to 40 minutes, until golden. Serve hot.

Nutrition Facts

Per Serving:

415.9 calories; protein 4g 8% DV; carbohydrates 58.2g 19% DV; fat 19.3g 30% DV; cholesterol 31.1mg 10% DV; sodium 641.3mg 26% DV.

Apple Honey Bundt Cake

Prep: 20 mins **Cook:** 55 mins **Total:** 1 hr 15 mins **Servings:** 12 **Yield:** 1 9-inch Bundt cake

Ingredients

- 1 cup white sugar
- 1 cup vegetable oil
- 2 large eggs eggs
- ¾ cup honey
- 1 teaspoon vanilla extract
- 2 ½ cups all-purpose flour
- 1 teaspoon baking powder
- 1 teaspoon baking soda
- 1 teaspoon salt
- 1 teaspoon ground cinnamon
- ¼ teaspoon ground allspice
- 3 medium (2-3/4" dia) (approx 3 per lb)s apples - peeled, cored and shredded
- ¾ cup chopped walnuts

Directions

Step 1

Preheat the oven to 325 degrees F (165 degrees C). Grease and flour a 9-inch Bundt pan or 2 loaf pans.

Step 2

In a large bowl, stir together the sugar and oil. Beat in the eggs until light, then stir in the honey and vanilla. Combine the flour, baking powder, baking soda, salt, cinnamon and allspice; stir into the batter just until moistened. Fold in the apples and nuts. Transfer batter to prepared pan or pans (see Cook's Note).

Step 3

Bake Bundt cake until a toothpick inserted into the crown comes out clean, about one hour. (Start checking for doneness after 50 minutes.) Let cool for 10 to 15 minutes before inverting onto a plate and tapping out of the pan. If desired, dust with confectioners' sugar, sprinkle with cinnamon, or drizzle with warm honey before serving.

Cook's Notes:

If you're baking the cake in loaf pans, reduce baking time to 45 minutes, or until a tester inserted in the center of each pan comes out clean.

You can substitute pecans for the walnuts, if you like.

Nutrition Facts

Per Serving:

463.8 calories; protein 5g 10% DV; carbohydrates 60.2g 19% DV; fat 24.1g 37% DV; cholesterol 31mg 10% DV; sodium 352.9mg 14% DV.

Chef John's Shepherd's Pie

Prep: 15 mins **Cook:** 55 mins **Additional:** 15 mins **Total:** 1 hr 25 mins **Servings:** 8 **Yield:** 8 servings

Ingredients

- 1 ¼ pounds Yukon Gold potatoes, peeled and cubed
- 3 cloves garlic, halved
- 1 pound lean ground beef
- 2 tablespoons flour
- ¾ cup beef broth
- 3 tablespoons ketchup
- 4 cups frozen mixed vegetables
- ½ teaspoon black pepper
- ½ cup shredded Cheddar cheese, divided
- ¾ cup light sour cream
- 1 teaspoon salt

Directions

Step 1

Place cubed potatoes and garlic in a large pot with enough water to cover. Bring to a boil over high heat; reduce heat to medium-low, cover, and simmer until tender, about 20 minutes.

Step 2

Preheat the oven to 375 degrees F (190 degrees C).

Step 3

Brown ground beef over medium heat in a skillet. Stir in flour, mixing with beef drippings.

Step 4

Add beef broth, ketchup and vegetables. Stir to combine. Cook for 5 minutes, until thick.

Step 5

Transfer beef mixture into an oven-proof casserole dish.

Step 6

Drain potatoes and smash them a little bit before adding 1/4 cup of grated cheese and sour cream. Mash together until smooth.

Step 7

Spoon potatoes onto the middle of the meat mixture. With a fork, spread potatoes from the center to the edges to form the top layer.

Step 8

Sprinkle with remaining 1/4 cup of grated cheese.

Step 9

Bake in the preheated oven for 20-25 minutes, or until cheese is melted and golden. Let cool 15 minutes before serving.

Nutrition Facts

Per Serving:

311.4 calories; protein 16.2g 32% DV; carbohydrates 23.5g 8% DV; fat 17.2g 27% DV; cholesterol 58.8mg 20% DV; sodium 546.4mg 22% DV.

Chocolate Chip Pumpkin Bread

Prep: 30 mins **Cook:** 1 hr **Total:** 1 hr 30 mins **Servings:** 36 **Yield:** 3 loaves

Ingredients

- 3 cups white sugar
- 1 (15 ounce) can pumpkin puree
- 1 cup vegetable oil
- ⅔ cup water
- 4 large eggs eggs
- 3 ½ cups all-purpose flour
- 1 tablespoon ground cinnamon
- 1 tablespoon ground nutmeg

- 2 teaspoons baking soda
- 1 ½ teaspoons salt
- 1 cup miniature semisweet chocolate chips
- ½ cup chopped walnuts

Directions

Step 1

Preheat oven to 350 degrees F (175 degrees C). Grease and flour three 1 pound size coffee cans, or three 9x5 inch loaf pans.

Step 2

In a large bowl, combine sugar, pumpkin, oil, water, and eggs. Beat until smooth. Blend in flour, cinnamon, nutmeg, baking soda, and salt. Fold in chocolate chips and nuts. Fill cans 1/2 to 3/4 full.

Step 3

Bake for 1 hour, or until an inserted knife comes out clean. Cool on wire racks before removing from cans or pans.

Nutrition Facts

Per Serving:

210.2 calories; protein 2.6g 5% DV; carbohydrates 30.5g 10% DV; fat 9.4g 15% DV; cholesterol 20.7mg 7% DV; sodium 204.1mg 8% DV.

Easy Chicken Marsala

Prep: 15 mins **Cook:** 25 mins **Total:** 40 mins **Servings:** 4 **Yield:** 4 servings

Ingredients

- 4 breast half, bone and skin removed (blank)s skinless, boneless chicken breast halves
- ¼ cup chopped green onion
- 1 cup sliced fresh mushrooms
- ⅓ cup Marsala wine
- salt and pepper to taste
- ⅓ cup heavy cream
- ⅛ cup milk

Directions

Step 1

Saute chicken in a large skillet for 15 to 20 minutes, or until cooked through and juices run clear.

Step 2

Add green onion and mushrooms and saute until soft, then add Marsala wine and bring to a boil.

Step 3

Boil for 2 to 4 minutes, seasoning with salt and pepper to taste. Stir in cream and milk and simmer until heated through, about 5 minutes.

Nutrition Facts

Per Serving:

240.9 calories; protein 28.4g 57% DV; carbohydrates 4.9g 2% DV; fat 9g 14% DV; cholesterol 96.2mg 32% DV; sodium 90.8mg 4% DV.

Easiest Eggplant

Prep: 10 mins **Cook:** 45 mins **Total:** 55 mins **Servings:** 6 **Yield:** 6 servings

Ingredients

- 1 medium eggplant, peeled and sliced into 1/2 inch rounds
- 4 tablespoons mayonnaise, or as needed
- ½ cup seasoned bread crumbs

Directions

Step 1

Preheat the oven to 350 degrees F. Line a baking sheet with aluminum foil.

Step 2

Place the bread crumbs in a shallow dish. Coat each slice of eggplant on both sides with mayonnaise. Press into the bread crumbs to coat. Place coated eggplant slices on the prepared baking sheet.

Step 3

Bake for 20 minutes in the preheated oven, until golden brown. Flip slices over, and cook for an additional 20 to 25 minutes to brown the other side.

Nutrition Facts

Per Serving:

126.3 calories; protein 2.4g 5% DV; carbohydrates 12.3g 4% DV; fat 8g 12% DV; cholesterol 3.6mg 1% DV; sodium 230mg 9% DV.

Fresh Apple Walnut Cake

Prep: 25 mins **Cook:** 45 mins **Total:** 1 hr 10 mins **Servings:** 12 **Yield:** 1 - 9x13 inch pan

Ingredients

- 3 cups all-purpose flour
- 1 teaspoon baking soda
- 1 teaspoon ground cinnamon
- ½ teaspoon salt
- 3 medium (2-3/4" dia) (approx 3 per lb)s apples - peeled, cored and sliced

- 1 cup white sugar
- 1 cup brown sugar
- 1 ¼ cups vegetable oil
- 2 large eggs eggs
- 2 teaspoons vanilla extract
- 1 cup chopped walnuts

Directions

Step 1

Preheat oven to 350 degrees F (175 degrees C). Grease and flour a 9x13 inch pan. Sift together the flour, baking soda, cinnamon and salt. Set aside.

Step 2

Combine the apples and the white sugar; set aside. In a large bowl, mix together the brown sugar, oil, eggs and vanilla. Stir in the apple mixture, then the flour mixture. Fold in the walnuts.

Step 3

Pour batter into prepared pan. Bake in the preheated oven for 45 minutes, or until a toothpick inserted into the center of the cake comes out clean. Allow to cool.

Nutrition Facts

Per Serving:

544.8 calories; protein 5.9g 12% DV; carbohydrates 64.9g 21% DV; fat 30.3g 47% DV; cholesterol 31mg 10% DV; sodium 219.8mg 9% DV.

Holiday Chicken Salad

Prep: 15 mins **Total:** 15 mins **Servings:** 12 **Yield:** 12 servings

Ingredients

- 4 cups cubed, cooked chicken meat
- 1 cup mayonnaise
- 1 teaspoon paprika
- 1 ½ cups dried cranberries
- 1 cup chopped celery
- 2 medium (4-1/8" long)s green onions, chopped
- ½ cup minced green bell pepper
- 1 cup chopped pecans
- 1 teaspoon seasoning salt
- ground black pepper to taste

Directions

Step 1

In a medium bowl, mix together mayonnaise with paprika and seasoned salt. Blend in dried cranberries, celery, bell pepper, onion, and nuts. Add chopped chicken, and mix well. Season with black pepper to taste. Chill 1 hour.

Nutrition Facts

Per Serving:

315.4 calories; protein 13.9g 28% DV; carbohydrates 15.2g 5% DV; fat 23.1g 36% DV; cholesterol 42mg 14% DV; sodium 213.1mg 9% DV.

Easy Canned Venison

Prep: 15 mins **Cook:** 1 hr 15 mins **Additional:** 4 hrs **Total:** 5 hrs 30 mins **Servings:** 4 **Yield:** 1 pint jar

Ingredients

- 1 pound cubed lean venison
- 1 teaspoon salt
- ¼ teaspoon ground black pepper
- 1 teaspoon minced garlic
- 4 slices onion
- 1 tablespoon minced green bell pepper

Directions

Step 1

Place the venison into a large bowl. Sprinkle with salt, pepper, and garlic; toss to combine. Place venison into canning jar along with onion and bell pepper. Jars should be filled to within 1/2 inch of the top. Wipe rim with a clean, damp cloth, and seal with lid and ring.

Step 2

Place jar into a pressure canner filled with water according to manufacturer's directions. Affix lid and bring to a boil with the pressure valve open. Boil for 5 minutes before closing the pressure valve. Bring to a pressure of 10 psi, then reduce heat in order to maintain this pressure. Process for 75 minutes, watching gauge closely so the pressure stays at 10 psi. After 75 minutes, turn off heat and allow the canner to cool until the gauge reads 0 psi.

Step 3

Once the pressure has subsided and the canner is safe to open, remove the jar to cool on a rack. The jar will seal with a pop as it cools; refrigerate the jar if it does not seal. Properly sealed jars may be stored in a cool, dark area.

Nutrition Facts

Per Serving:

128.2 calories; protein 23.3g 47% DV; carbohydrates 1.7g 1% DV; fat 2.5g 4% DV; cholesterol 85.5mg 29% DV; sodium 610.4mg 24% DV.

Easy Pumpkin Pie Squares

Prep: 20 mins **Cook:** 35 mins **Total:** 55 mins **Servings:** 24 **Yield:** 1 - 9x13 inch dish

Ingredients

- ½ cup butter, softened
- ½ cup brown sugar
- 1 cup all-purpose flour
- ½ cup rolled oats
- 2 large eggs eggs
- ¾ cup white sugar
- 1 (15 ounce) can pumpkin
- 1 (12 fluid ounce) can evaporated milk
- ½ teaspoon salt
- 1 teaspoon ground cinnamon
- ½ teaspoon ground ginger
- ¼ teaspoon ground cloves

Directions

Step 1

Preheat oven to 350 degrees F (175 degrees C).

Step 2

In a medium bowl, cream together butter and brown sugar. Mix in flour. Fold in oats. Press into a 9x13 inch baking dish.

Step 3

Bake in preheated oven 15 minutes, until set.

Step 4

In a large bowl, beat eggs with white sugar. Beat in pumpkin and evaporated milk. Mix in salt, cinnamon, ginger and cloves. Pour over baked crust.

Step 5

Bake in preheated oven 20 minutes, until set. Let cool before cutting into squares.

Nutrition Facts

Per Serving:

134.3 calories; protein 2.7g 5% DV; carbohydrates 18.9g 6% DV; fat 5.7g 9% DV; cholesterol 30.2mg 10% DV; sodium 100.5mg 4% DV.

Apple Slab Pie

Prep: 30 mins Cook: 1 hr Total: 1 hr 30 mins Servings: 15 Yield: 1 - 10x15 inch pie

Ingredients

- 1 ½ cups all-purpose flour
- 1 ½ tablespoons white sugar
- ½ cup shortening
- ¼ teaspoon salt
- ½ teaspoon baking powder
- 2 large egg yolks egg yolks, beaten
- 4 tablespoons water
- 8 medium (2-3/4" dia) (approx 3 per lb)s apples - peeled, cored and cut into thin wedges
- 2 tablespoons lemon juice
- 2 tablespoons all-purpose flour
- 1 ¾ cups white sugar
- ½ teaspoon ground cinnamon
- 2 tablespoons butter
- 1 cup all-purpose flour
- 1 teaspoon ground cinnamon
- ⅔ cup brown sugar
- ⅔ cup butter

Directions

Step 1

Preheat oven to 350 degrees F (175 degrees C.) In a large bowl, combine flour sugar, salt and baking powder. Cut in shortening until mixture resembles coarse crumbs. Mix egg yolk and water together and mix into flour until it forms a ball. Roll out to fit the bottom of a 10x15 inch pan.

Step 2

In a large bowl, combine apples, lemon juice, 2 tablespoons flour, sugar and cinnamon. Pour filling into pie crust and dot with 2 tablespoons butter.

Step 3

In a medium bowl, combine 1 cup flour, 1 teaspoon cinnamon, 2/3 cup brown sugar and 2/3 cup butter. Cut in the butter until crumbly, then sprinkle over apples.

Step 4

Bake in the preheated oven for 60 minutes, or until topping is golden brown.

Nutrition Facts

Per Serving:

404.7 calories; protein 2.9g 6% DV; carbohydrates 61.5g 20% DV; fat 17.5g 27% DV; cholesterol 53.1mg 18% DV; sodium 124.9mg 5% DV.

Apple Slab Pie

Prep: 30 mins **Cook:** 1 hr **Total:** 1 hr 30 mins **Servings:** 15 **Yield:** 1 - 10x15 inch pie

Ingredients

- 1 ½ cups all-purpose flour
- 1 ½ tablespoons white sugar
- ½ cup shortening
- ¼ teaspoon salt
- ½ teaspoon baking powder
- 2 large egg yolks egg yolks, beaten
- 4 tablespoons water
- 8 medium (2-3/4" dia) (approx 3 per lb)s apples - peeled, cored and cut into thin wedges
- 2 tablespoons lemon juice
- 2 tablespoons all-purpose flour
- 1 ¾ cups white sugar
- ½ teaspoon ground cinnamon
- 2 tablespoons butter
- 1 cup all-purpose flour
- 1 teaspoon ground cinnamon
- ⅔ cup brown sugar
- ⅔ cup butter

Directions

Step 1

Preheat oven to 350 degrees F (175 degrees C.) In a large bowl, combine flour sugar, salt and baking powder. Cut in shortening until mixture resembles coarse crumbs. Mix egg yolk and water together and mix into flour until it forms a ball. Roll out to fit the bottom of a 10x15 inch pan.

Step 2

In a large bowl, combine apples, lemon juice, 2 tablespoons flour, sugar and cinnamon. Pour filling into pie crust and dot with 2 tablespoons butter.

Step 3

In a medium bowl, combine 1 cup flour, 1 teaspoon cinnamon, 2/3 cup brown sugar and 2/3 cup butter. Cut in the butter until crumbly, then sprinkle over apples.

Step 4

Bake in the preheated oven for 60 minutes, or until topping is golden brown.

Nutrition Facts

Per Serving:

404.7 calories; protein 2.9g 6% DV; carbohydrates 61.5g 20% DV; fat 17.5g 27% DV; cholesterol 53.1mg 18% DV; sodium 124.9mg 5% DV.

Pumpkin Dump Cake

Prep: 10 mins **Cook:** 50 mins **Total:** 1 hr **Servings:** 12 **Yield:** 1 - 9x13 inch pan

Ingredients

- 1 (29 ounce) can pumpkin puree
- 3 large eggs eggs
- ½ cup packed brown sugar
- ½ cup white sugar
- 1 (12 fluid ounce) can evaporated milk
- 1 teaspoon ground cinnamon
- ½ teaspoon ground ginger
- ¼ teaspoon ground cloves
- ½ teaspoon salt
- 1 (18.25 ounce) package spice cake mix
- ½ cup coarsely chopped pecans
- ½ cup melted butter

Directions

Step 1

Preheat oven to 350 degrees F (175 degrees C). Grease a 9x13 inch pan.

Step 2

In a large bowl, combine pumpkin puree, eggs, brown sugar, white sugar and milk. Stir in cinnamon, ginger, cloves and salt. Pour into pan. Sprinkle dry cake mix evenly over the pumpkin filling. Sprinkle pecans over the cake mix. Drizzle melted butter over all.

Step 3

Bake in the preheated oven for 50 to 60 minutes, or until the edges are lightly browned. Allow to cool.

Nutrition Facts

Per Serving:

434.2 calories; protein 7.6g 15% DV; carbohydrates 58.4g 19% DV; fat 20.1g 31% DV; cholesterol 76mg 25% DV; sodium 658.1mg 26% DV.

Lime Gelatin Salad I

Prep: 20 mins **Cook:** 5 mins **Additional:** 4 hrs **Total:** 4 hrs 25 mins **Servings:** 10 **Yield:** 10 servings

Ingredients

- 1 cup boiling water
- 1 (6 ounce) package lime flavored Jell-O mix
- 1 (20 ounce) can crushed pineapple, drained with juice reserved
- 1 (8 ounce) package cream cheese, softened
- 2 cups heavy cream
- 1 cup chopped pecans

Directions

Step 1

In a large bowl, pour 1 cup boiling water over the gelatin mix. Stir until dissolved, then stir in 1/2 cup pineapple juice. Refrigerate until thickened but not set, about 1 hour.

Step 2

Meanwhile, place crushed pineapple and remaining juice in a small saucepan. Bring to a boil, reduce heat, and simmer for about 5 minutes. Remove from heat, and cool to room temperature.

Step 3

In a large bowl, blend softened cream cheese and lime gelatin until smooth. Mix in the cooled pineapple. In a medium bowl, whip cream until soft peaks form. Fold into gelatin mixture. Fold in chopped nuts. Pour into a pretty crystal bowl, and refrigerate for at least 4 hours, or until set.

Nutrition Facts

Per Serving:

412.4 calories; protein 5.4g 11% DV; carbohydrates 26.7g 9% DV; fat 33.3g 51% DV; cholesterol 89.9mg 30% DV; sodium 161.3mg 7% DV.

Bread and Celery Stuffing

Prep: 20 mins **Cook:** 40 mins **Additional:** 1 hr **Total:** 2 hrs **Servings:** 10 **Yield:** 10 servings

Ingredients

- 1 (1 pound) loaf sliced white bread
- ¾ cup butter or margarine
- 1 onion, chopped
- 4 stalks celery, chopped
- 2 teaspoons poultry seasoning
- ½ teaspoon salt and pepper to taste
- 1 cup chicken broth

Directions

Step 1

Let bread slices air dry for 1 to 2 hours, then cut into cubes.

Step 2

In a Dutch oven, melt butter or margarine over medium heat. Cook onion and celery until soft. Season with poultry seasoning, salt, and pepper. Stir in bread cubes until evenly coated. Moisten with chicken broth; mix well.

Step 3

Chill, and use as a stuffing for turkey, or bake in a buttered casserole dish at 350 degrees F (175 degrees C) for 30 to 40 minutes.

Nutrition Facts

Per Serving:

254.4 calories; protein 4.4g 9% DV; carbohydrates 24.7g 8% DV; fat 15.5g 24% DV; cholesterol 36.6mg 12% DV; sodium 613.1mg 25% DV.

Gorgonzola Cream Sauce

Prep: 15 mins **Cook:** 25 mins **Total:** 40 mins **Servings:** 6 **Yield:** 6 servings

Ingredients

- 1 cup heavy whipping cream
- 1 pinch salt and freshly ground black pepper to taste
- 1 pinch cayenne pepper, or to taste
- 6 ounces dry miniature ravioli
- 3 ounces crumbled Gorgonzola cheese
- 2 tablespoons chopped Italian flat leaf parsley
- 2 tablespoons freshly grated Parmesan cheese
- ½ apple, diced
- ¼ cup chopped toasted walnuts
- 1 teaspoon chopped Italian flat leaf parsley

Directions

Step 1

Place a heavy skillet over medium heat. Pour cream into skillet, bring to a simmer, and cook cream until it reduces by half, about 8 minutes, stirring occasionally. Season with salt, black pepper, and cayenne pepper.

Step 2

Bring a pot of salted water to a boil. Pour dried ravioli into boiling water and cook, stirring occasionally, until pasta is tender, 16 to 18 minutes. Drain pasta, reserving a cup of pasta water.

Step 3

Gently fold cooked ravioli into cream sauce and turn heat to low. Mix in Gorgonzola cheese, stirring gently until melted. If sauce is too thick, thin it with a little pasta cooking water.

Step 4

Stir in 2 tablespoons parsley and Parmesan cheese. Transfer to a serving bowl and sprinkle with diced apple, walnuts, and 1 teaspoon parsley.

Cook's Note:

If you use fresh ravioli or tortellini, use double the amount of pasta: 12 ounces instead of 6.

Nutrition Facts

Per Serving:

299.7 calories; protein 8.5g 17% DV; carbohydrates 12.6g 4% DV; fat 24.4g 38% DV; cholesterol 81.8mg 27% DV; sodium 257.7mg 10% DV.

Creamy Mushroom Meatloaf

Prep: 15 mins **Cook:** 2 hrs **Total:** 2 hrs 15 mins **Servings:** 8 **Yield:** 8 servings

Ingredients

- ¼ cup butter
- 2 cups shiitake mushrooms, sliced
- 1 pinch salt
- 1 sprig fresh rosemary, chopped
- 3 tablespoons all-purpose flour
- 2 ½ cups beef broth
- 1 pinch salt and pepper to taste
- ½ cup heavy cream
- 1 (2 1/2 pound) uncooked prepared beef, veal and pork meatloaf

Directions

Step 1

Preheat the oven to 325 degrees F (165 degrees C).

Step 2

Melt butter in an oven-safe skillet over medium-high heat. Stir in mushrooms and a pinch of salt; cook and stir until mushrooms begin to brown, about 5 minutes.

Step 3

Stir in fresh rosemary. Add flour and stir to coat the mushrooms; cook and stir for about 3 minutes.

Step 4

Whisk in beef broth, 1/2 cup at a time, whisking constantly to prevent lumps.

Step 5

Turn heat to high and bring the sauce to a simmer. Simmer a few minutes until sauce starts to thicken. Season with salt and pepper to taste.

Step 6

Remove from heat and stir in heavy cream.
Step 7

Slide prepared meatloaf into the sauce. Spoon sauce over the top of the meatloaf.
Step 8

Bake in the preheated oven until no longer pink in the center, about 1 1/2 hours. An instant-read thermometer inserted into the center should read at least 160 degrees F (70 degrees C).
Step 9

Remove pan from the oven and gently remove meatloaf to a serving platter.
Step 10

Skim off any extra fat from the surface of the sauce.
Step 11

Bring the sauce to a boil over medium-high heat to reduce until thick, about 5 minutes.
Cook's Notes:
Use any recipe you like for the meatloaf. Nutritional information is for a 2 1/2 pound beef, veal and pork meatloaf.
Try this recipe for Classic Meatloaf, which calls for ground chuck. Or use 1.5 pounds ground beef, 1 pound ground pork.
Using cold beef broth keeps the flour from forming lumps.
Nutrition Facts
Per Serving:
323.9 calories; protein 27.9g 56% DV; carbohydrates 13.6g 4% DV; fat 16.5g 25% DV; cholesterol 138.6mg 46% DV; sodium 501.1mg 20% DV.

Ranch, Bacon, and Parmesan Pasta Salad

Prep: 15 mins **Additional:** 2 hrs 30 mins **Total:** 2 hrs 45 mins **Servings:** 6 **Yield:** 6 servings
Ingredients
- 1 (16 ounce) package farfalle (bow tie) pasta
- 1 cup prepared ranch dressing
- 6 slices bacon
- ½ cup shredded Parmesan cheese
- 1 carrot, peeled and diced
- 1 stalk celery, diced
- 1 red onion, diced

Directions

Step 1

Fill a large pot with lightly salted water and bring to a rolling boil over high heat. Once the water is boiling, stir in the bow tie pasta and return to a boil. Cook the pasta uncovered, stirring occasionally, until the pasta has cooked through, but is still firm to the bite, about 12 minutes. Drain well in a colander set in the sink. Transfer to a bowl, and refrigerate until cool, at least 30 minutes.

Step 2

Meanwhile, place the bacon in a large, deep skillet, and cook over medium-high heat, turning occasionally, until evenly browned, about 10 minutes. Drain the bacon slices on a paper towel-lined plate, let cool, and chop.

Step 3

In a large salad bowl, stir together the ranch dressing, bacon, Parmesan cheese, carrot, celery, and red onion until well combined. Lightly stir in the cooled pasta to coat with dressing, and refrigerate 2 hours to blend flavors before serving.

Cook's Note

Lettuce or cabbage can also be substituted for the pasta in this recipe for a lighter summer salad with crunch.

Nutrition Facts

Per Serving:

583.8 calories; protein 17.7g 35% DV; carbohydrates 62.8g 20% DV; fat 28.3g 44% DV; cholesterol 26.8mg 9% DV; sodium 712.7mg 29% DV.

Pumpkin Pie Spice I

Prep: 1 min **Total:** 1 min **Servings:** 8 **Yield:** cup

Ingredients

- ¼ cup ground cinnamon
- 4 teaspoons ground nutmeg
- 4 teaspoons ground ginger
- 1 tablespoon ground allspice

Directions

Step 1

Combine cinnamon, nutmeg, ginger, and allspice together in a bowl. Store in air-tight container.

Nutrition Facts

Per Serving:

21.5 calories; protein 0.4g 1% DV; carbohydrates 4.7g 2% DV; fat 0.7g 1% DV; cholesterolmg; sodium 1.5mg.

Roasted Garlic Parmesan Mashed Potatoes

Prep: 15 mins **Cook:** 1 hr **Total:** 1 hr 15 mins **Servings:** 8 **Yield:** 8 servings

Ingredients

- 6 cloves garlic, peeled
- ¼ cup olive oil
- 7 medium (2-1/4" to 3" dia, raw)s baking potatoes, peeled and cubed
- ½ cup milk
- ¼ cup grated Parmesan cheese
- 2 tablespoons butter
- ½ teaspoon salt
- ¼ teaspoon ground black pepper

Directions

Step 1

Preheat oven to 350 degrees F (175 degrees C).

Step 2

Place garlic cloves in a small baking dish. Drizzle with olive oil, cover, and bake 45 minutes, or until golden brown.

Step 3

Bring a large pot of lightly salted water to boil. Add potatoes, and cook until tender but firm. Drain, and transfer to a large mixing bowl.

Step 4

Place roasted garlic, milk, Parmesan cheese, and butter into the bowl with the potatoes. Season with salt and pepper. Beat to desired consistency with an electric mixer.

Nutrition Facts

Per Serving:

250.6 calories; protein 5.4g 11% DV; carbohydrates 34.2g 11% DV; fat 10.8g 17% DV; cholesterol 11.1mg 4% DV; sodium 222mg 9% DV.

Apple Scones

Prep: 15 mins **Cook:** 15 mins **Total:** 30 mins **Servings:** 12 **Yield:** 12 scones

Ingredients

- 2 cups all-purpose flour
- ¼ cup white sugar
- 2 teaspoons baking powder

- ½ teaspoon baking soda
- ½ teaspoon salt
- ¼ cup butter, chilled
- 1 apple - peeled, cored and shredded
- ½ cup milk
- 2 tablespoons milk
- 2 tablespoons white sugar
- ½ teaspoon ground cinnamon

Directions

Step 1

Measure flour, sugar, baking powder, soda, and salt into a large bowl. Cut in butter or margarine until crumbly. Add shredded apple and milk. Stir to form a soft dough.

Step 2

Turn dough out onto a lightly floured surface. Knead gently 8 to 10 times. Pat into two 6-inch circles. Place on greased baking sheet. Brush tops with milk, and sprinkle with sugar and cinnamon. Score each into 6 pie-shaped wedges.

Step 3

Bake at 425 degrees F (220 degrees C) for 15 minutes, or until browned and risen. Serve warm with butter.

Nutrition Facts

Per Serving:

146.9 calories; protein 2.6g 5% DV; carbohydrates 24.6g 8% DV; fat 4.3g 7% DV; cholesterol 11.2mg 4% DV; sodium 263.6mg 11% DV.

Easy Apple Rhubarb Jam

Cook: 25 mins **Total:** 25 mins **Servings:** 48 **Yield:** 6 cups

Ingredients

- 3 cups diced rhubarb
- 3 cups diced peeled apples
- 2 cups white sugar
- ½ cup water
- 1 tablespoon ground cinnamon
- 1 (2 ounce) package dry pectin

Directions

Step 1

In a large saucepan mix together the rhubarb, apples, sugar, water and cinnamon. Bring to a boil, then cook over medium heat for 20 minutes or until the fruit is soft. Stir in the pectin and boil for 5 minutes.
Step 2

Ladle into sterile jars, wipe rims with a clean cloth or paper towel, and seal with new lids. Process in a bath of simmering water for at least 10 minutes, or as recommended by your local extension if you are at a high altitude. Store unopened jars in a cool dark place. Refrigerate jam after opening.

Cook's Note:

To make strawberry-rhubarb jam, replace the apples with three cups of strawberries and the pectin with one 6-ounce box of strawberry gelatin.

Nutrition Facts

Per Serving:

38.3 calories; protein 0.1g; carbohydrates 9.9g 3% DV; fatg; cholesterolmg; sodium 0.5mg.

Grandma's Fresh Apple Cake

Prep: 25 mins **Cook:** 1 hr **Total:** 1 hr 25 mins **Servings:** 12 **Yield:** 1 cake

Ingredients

- 1 cup all-purpose flour
- 1 teaspoon baking soda
- 1 teaspoon ground cinnamon
- ½ teaspoon salt
- 1 cup white sugar
- 1 egg
- ¼ cup vegetable oil
- 2 cups peeled and chopped apple
- ½ cup chopped walnuts
- ½ cup raisins

Directions

Step 1

Preheat oven to 350 degrees F (175 degrees C). Grease and flour a fluted tube pan (such as Bundt).

Step 2

Sift flour, baking soda, cinnamon, and salt together in a bowl. Set aside.

Step 3

Mix sugar, egg, and oil together in another bowl. Stir in the flour mixture just until combined; fold in apple, walnuts, and raisins.

Step 4

Bake in the preheated oven until a toothpick inserted into the cake comes out clean, about 1 hour.

Cook's Note:

You can use dates instead of raisins, and any kind of chopped nut that you prefer.

Nutrition Facts

Per Serving:

212.6 calories; protein 2.6g 5% DV; carbohydrates 33.8g 11% DV; fat 8.3g 13% DV; cholesterol 15.5mg 5% DV; sodium 208.9mg 8% DV.

Apple and Tomato Chutney

Prep: 30 mins **Cook:** 3 hrs 30 mins **Total:** 4 hrs **Servings:** 75 **Yield:** 1 gallon

Ingredients

- 2 pounds apples - peeled, cored and sliced
- 2 cups water
- 1 tablespoon mustard seed
- 2 pounds tomatoes, sliced
- 2 large onions, chopped
- 1 clove garlic, chopped
- ½ cup sultana raisins
- ¾ cup white sugar
- 5 teaspoons curry powder
- 1 teaspoon cayenne pepper
- 4 teaspoons salt
- 2 ½ cups malt vinegar

Directions

Step 1

Place apples and water in a large saucepan. Bring to a boil, reduce heat, and cook 25 minutes, or until apples are tender, stirring occasionally. Add more water as necessary to keep the apples simmering.

Step 2

Wrap mustard seed in cheesecloth, and place with apples. Mix tomatoes, onions, garlic, sultanas, sugar, curry powder, cayenne pepper, salt and vinegar into saucepan. Stir until sugar has dissolved.

Step 3

Bring the mixture to a boil. Reduce heat, and simmer 3 hours, stirring occassionally, until a thick chutney remains. Remove and discard wrapped mustard seed. Seal chutney in sterile containers until serving.

Nutrition Facts

Per Serving:

24.7 calories; protein 0.3g 1% DV; carbohydrates 6.2g 2% DV; fat 0.1g; cholesterolmg; sodium 128.1mg 5% DV.

Simple Swiss Chard

Prep: 10 mins **Cook:** 10 mins **Total:** 20 mins **Servings:** 2 **Yield:** 2 servings

Ingredients

- 2 tablespoons extra-virgin olive oil
- 4 cloves garlic, minced
- 1 bunch Swiss chard, stalks discarded, leaves cut into wide ribbons
- ¼ cup balsamic vinegar
- 1 pinch salt and pepper to taste

Directions

Step 1

Heat the olive oil on a large skillet over medium heat. Stir in the garlic and cook until tender and aromatic, about 2 minutes. Add the Swiss chard and balsamic vinegar; cook and stir until the chard is wilted and tender, about 5 minutes. Season with salt and pepper and serve.

Nutrition Facts

Per Serving:

171.5 calories; protein 2.5g 5% DV; carbohydrates 10.9g 4% DV; fat 13.8g 21% DV; cholesterolmg; sodium 250.5mg 10% DV.

Apple Stuffed Pork Chops

Servings: 6 **Yield:** 6 chops

Ingredients

- 1 tablespoon chopped onion
- ¼ cup butter
- 3 cups fresh bread crumbs
- 2 cups chopped apples
- ¼ cup chopped celery
- 2 teaspoons chopped fresh parsley
- ¼ teaspoon salt
- 6 raw chop with refuse, 106 g; yields excluding refuses (1 1/4 inch) thick pork chops
- salt and pepper to taste
- 1 tablespoon vegetable oil

Directions

Step 1

Preheat oven to 350 degrees F (175 degrees C).

Step 2

In a large skillet saute onion in butter or margarine until tender. Remove from heat. Add the bread crumbs, apples, celery, parsley and salt. Mix all together. Cut a large pocket in the side of each pork chop; season inside and out with salt and pepper to taste. Spoon apple mixture loosely into pockets.

Step 3

In skillet, heat oil to medium high and brown chops on both sides. Place browned chops in an ungreased 9x13 inch baking dish. Cover with aluminum foil and bake in the preheated oven for 30 minutes. Remove cover and bake for 30 minutes longer or until juices run clear.

Nutrition Facts

Per Serving:

483.2 calories; protein 32.2g 65% DV; carbohydrates 45g 15% DV; fat 18.9g 29% DV; cholesterol 89.7mg 30% DV; sodium 625.7mg 25% DV.

Country Banana Bread

Prep: 20 mins **Cook:** 40 mins **Total:** 1 hr **Servings:** 9 **Yield:** 8 to 10 servings

Ingredients

- 1 (18.25 ounce) package yellow cake mix
- 3 large eggs eggs
- 1 ⅓ cups vegetable oil
- 4 medium (7" to 7-7/8" long)s bananas, mashed

Directions

Step 1

Preheat oven to 350 degrees F (175 degrees C). Grease a 9x13 inch pan.

Step 2

In a mixing bowl, combine cake mix, eggs, oil, and bananas. Pour mixture into the prepared pan.

Step 3

Bake in preheated 350 degrees F (175 degrees C) for 35 to 40 minutes.

Nutrition Facts

Per Serving:

606.8 calories; protein 5.2g 10% DV; carbohydrates 57g 18% DV; fat 41.1g 63% DV; cholesterol 63.1mg 21% DV; sodium 401.3mg 16% DV.

Danish Pastry Apple Bars

Prep: 30 mins **Cook:** 1 hr **Total:** 1 hr 30 mins **Servings:** 12 **Yield:** 1 9x13-inch pan

Ingredients

- 2 ½ cups all-purpose flour
- 1 teaspoon salt
- 1 cup shortening
- 1 egg yolk
- ½ cup milk
- 10 medium (2-3/4" dia) (approx 3 per lb)s apples - peeled, cored and thinly sliced
- ½ cup light brown sugar
- ¼ cup white sugar
- ½ teaspoon ground cinnamon
- ¼ teaspoon ground nutmeg
- 1 egg white

Directions

Step 1

Preheat oven to 375 degrees F (190 degrees C.)

Step 2

In a large bowl, combine flour and salt. Cut in shortening until mixture resembles coarse crumbs. Beat egg yolk in measuring cup and add enough milk to make 2/3 cup total liquid. Stir into flour mixture until all flour is damp. Divide the dough in half. On floured surface, roll half the dough into a rectangle and fit into a 9x13 inch pan.

Step 3

In large bowl, combine apples, brown sugar, white sugar, cinnamon and nutmeg. Put apple mixture in pan. Roll out remaining dough and place over apples. Seal edges and cut slits in top dough. Beat egg white till frothy and brush on crust.

Step 4

Bake in the preheated oven for 50 minutes, or until golden brown.

Cook's Note:

I also use this recipe with a blueberry filling: 2 cups white sugar, 1/2 cup all-purpose flour, 1/2 teaspoon salt, and 1/2 teaspoon cinnamon.

Nutrition Facts

Per Serving:

356.1 calories; protein 3.9g 8% DV; carbohydrates 46.5g 15% DV; fat 18.1g 28% DV; cholesterol 17.9mg 6% DV; sodium 206.6mg 8% DV.

Absolute Stress

Prep: 5 mins **Total:** 5 mins **Servings:** 1 **Yield:** 1 serving

Ingredients

- 1 fluid ounce vodka
- 1 fluid ounce dark rum
- 1 fluid ounce peach schnapps
- 1 fluid ounce orange juice
- 1 fluid ounce cranberry juice

Directions

Step 1

In a cocktail shaker, combine vodka, rum, peach liqueur, orange juice and cranberry juice. Shake well.

Step 2

Pour over ice in a tall glass and garnish with a slice of orange and a cherry.

Nutrition Facts

Per Serving:

265.5 calories; protein 0.2g; carbohydrates 20.8g 7% DV; fat 0.2g; cholesterolmg; sodium 3.4mg.

Sheet Pan Roasted Vegetables

Prep: 30 mins **Cook:** 1 hr 30 mins **Total:** 2 hrs **Servings:** 24 **Yield:** 24 servings

Ingredients

- 8 medium (blank)s zucchini, peeled and chopped
- 1 eggplant, peeled and diced
- 8 medium (blank)s carrots, diced
- 16 eaches cherry tomatoes
- 2 medium (2-1/2" dia)s red onions, sliced
- 1 red bell pepper, sliced
- 1 yellow bell pepper, sliced
- ½ cup olive oil
- 1 teaspoon dried rosemary
- 1 teaspoon dried thyme
- 2 leaf (blank)s bay leaves, crushed
- 1 teaspoon dried oregano
- 2 cloves garlic, minced
- 2 tablespoons fresh lemon juice
- 1 teaspoon grated lemon zest

- salt and pepper to taste

Directions

Step 1

In a large bowl mix the zucchini, eggplant, carrots, tomatoes, onions and peppers with the oil, rosemary, thyme, bay leaves, oregano, garlic, lemon juice, lemon zest, salt and pepper. Cover and chill for at least 2 hours, and preferably overnight.

Step 2

Preheat oven to 400 degrees F (200 degrees C).

Step 3

On a large roasting pan, roast the vegetables, uncovered, for 20 minutes, or until the tomatoes have split and the edges of some of the vegetables are starting to crisp. Remove from the oven and stir before returning to the oven for another 20 minutes. At this time reduce heat to 200 degrees F (95 degrees C) and continue cooking until vegetables are tender, turning every 20 minutes.

Nutrition Facts

Per Serving:

71.9 calories; protein 1.5g 3% DV; carbohydrates 7.3g 2% DV; fat 4.7g 7% DV; cholesterolmg; sodium 11.1mg.

Feta Cheese Foldovers

Prep: 20 mins **Cook:** 20 mins **Total:** 40 mins **Servings:** 12 **Yield:** 12 servings

Ingredients

- 8 ounces feta cheese, crumbled
- 3 tablespoons finely chopped green onions
- 1 egg, beaten
- 1 (17.5 ounce) package frozen puff pastry, thawed
- 1 egg yolk, beaten with 1 teaspoon water

Directions

Step 1

Preheat oven to 375 degrees F (190 degrees C).

Step 2

In a small bowl, blend feta cheese, green onions, and egg. Cut pastry into 12 (3 inch) squares. Place a mounded tablespoon of feta mixture in the center of each square. Moisten edges with water, and fold pastry over filling to form a triangle. Press edges together firmly with a fork to seal. Lightly brush pastries with the egg yolk mixture.

Step 3

Bake for 20 minutes in the preheated oven, or until golden brown. Serve warm or at room temperature.

Nutrition Facts

Per Serving:

285.7 calories; protein 6.4g 13% DV; carbohydrates 19.4g 6% DV; fat 20.4g 31% DV; cholesterol 49.4mg 17% DV; sodium 319.3mg 13% DV.

Applesauce Doughnuts

Prep: 15 mins **Cook:** 15 mins **Total:** 30 mins **Servings:** 24 **Yield:** 4 dozen

Ingredients

- 2 quarts oil for frying
- 2 ¼ cups all-purpose flour
- 1 ½ teaspoons baking powder
- ½ teaspoon baking soda
- ½ teaspoon ground cinnamon
- ½ teaspoon nutmeg
- ¼ teaspoon ground cloves
- ¼ teaspoon salt
- ½ cup white sugar
- ¼ cup firmly packed light brown sugar
- 2 large eggs eggs
- 2 tablespoons vegetable oil
- ¼ cup milk
- 1 cup unsweetened applesauce
- ½ teaspoon vanilla extract

Directions

Step 1

Heat oil in deep-fryer to 375 degrees F (190 degrees C).

Step 2

Sift together flour, baking powder, baking soda, cinnamon, nutmeg, cloves and salt onto piece of waxed paper.

Step 3

In a large bowl, use an electric mixer at medium speed to beat together sugar, brown sugar and eggs until fluffy. Beat in 2 tablespoon oil. Stir flour mixture into egg mixture, alternately with milk, beginning and ending with dry ingredients, until well blended. Stir in applesauce and vanilla.

Step 4

Carefully drop batter by level tablespoons, 3 or 4 at a time, into hot oil. Do not overcrowd pan or oil may overflow. Fry, turning once with tongs, for 3 minutes or until golden. Transfer with tongs to paper toweling to drain. Cool completely.

Nutrition Facts

Per Serving:

154.8 calories; protein 1.8g 4% DV; carbohydrates 16.8g 5% DV; fat 9.1g 14% DV; cholesterol 15.7mg 5% DV; sodium 81mg 3% DV.

Savory Roasted Root Vegetables

Prep: 30 mins **Cook:** 45 mins **Total:** 1 hr 15 mins **Servings:** 6 **Yield:** 6 servings

Ingredients

- 1 cup diced, raw beet
- 4 medium (blank)s carrots, diced
- 1 onion, diced
- 2 cups diced potatoes
- 4 cloves garlic, minced
- ¼ cup canned garbanzo beans (chickpeas), drained
- 2 tablespoons olive oil
- 1 tablespoon dried thyme leaves
- 1 pinch salt and pepper to taste
- ⅓ cup dry white wine
- 1 cup torn beet greens

Directions

Step 1

Preheat an oven to 400 degrees F (200 degrees C).

Step 2

Place the beet, carrot, onion, potatoes, garlic, and garbanzo beans into a 9x13 inch baking dish. Drizzle with the olive oil, then season with thyme, salt, and pepper. Mix well.

Step 3

Bake, uncovered, in the preheated oven for 30 minutes, stirring once midway through baking. Remove the baking dish from the oven, and stir in the wine. Return to the oven, and bake until the wine has mostly evaporated and the vegetables are tender, about 15 minutes more. Stir in the beet greens, allowing them to wilt from the heat of the vegetables. Season to taste with salt and pepper before serving.

Nutrition Facts

Per Serving:

143 calories; protein 2.8g 6% DV; carbohydrates 20.8g 7% DV; fat 4.9g 8% DV; cholesterolmg; sodium 95.3mg 4% DV.

Best Ever Caramel Apple Crisp

Prep: 45 mins **Cook:** 55 mins **Total:** 1 hr 40 mins **Servings:** 12 **Yield:** 12 servings

Ingredients

Apple Filling:

- 5 large Granny Smith apples - peeled, cored, and thinly sliced
- ½ cup white sugar
- 1 tablespoon all-purpose flour
- ½ teaspoon ground cinnamon
- 1 tablespoon lemon juice
- ¼ cup water

Crumble:

- 1 ½ cups all-purpose flour
- 1 cup brown sugar
- 1 cup quick cooking oats
- 1 cup butter, softened
- Caramel Sauce:
- 1 (14 ounce) package individually wrapped caramels, unwrapped
- 1 (5 ounce) can evaporated milk

Directions

Step 1

Preheat oven to 350 F (175 degree C).

Step 2

In a medium size bowl, toss apples with sugar, flour, cinnamon, lemon juice, and water; spread evenly into a 8x8 inch pan. In another bowl, mix together flour, brown sugar, oats, and butter; spoon mixture evenly over apples.

Step 3

In a heavy sauce pan over low heat, melt the caramels with the evaporated milk. Heat , stirring frequently, until mixture has a smooth consistency. Drizzle the caramel sauce over the top of the crumble.

Step 4

Bake in preheated oven for about 45 minutes (apple mixture will bubble and topping will be golden brown).

Nutrition Facts

Per Serving:

502.2 calories; protein 5.3g 11% DV; carbohydrates 80.8g 26% DV; fat 19.5g 30% DV; cholesterol 46.3mg 15% DV; sodium 208.3mg 8% DV.

Chef John's Roasted Brussels Sprouts

Prep: 10 mins **Cook:** 35 mins **Total:** 45 mins **Servings:** 4 **Yield:** 4 servings

Ingredients

- 1 pound Brussels sprouts, trimmed and halved lengthwise
- ½ pound cipollini onions, stem and root ends trimmed
- 2 tablespoons butter
- 1 pinch salt and ground black pepper to taste
- 1 lemon, cut into wedges

Directions

Step 1

Preheat an oven to 450 degrees F (230 degrees C).

Step 2

Fill a large pot with water and bring to a rolling boil over high heat. Place Brussels sprouts in water and cook for 2 minutes. Remove sprouts from water and transfer to ice water to cool. Drain and pat dry. Set aside.

Step 3

Place onions in boiling water; cook until nearly tender, about 10 minutes. Remove from water, rinse with cold water, and pat dry. Set aside.

Step 4

Melt butter in an ovenproof skillet over medium heat. Stir in Brussels sprouts and onions; toss with butter to coat. Stir in salt and black pepper; cook for 2 minutes.

Step 5

Transfer skillet to the preheated oven and roast until golden and tender, 15 to 20 minutes. Garnish with lemon wedges and serve.

Nutrition Facts

Per Serving:

125.3 calories; protein 4.9g 10% DV; carbohydrates 17.8g 6% DV; fat 6.2g 10% DV; cholesterol 15.3mg 5% DV; sodium 70.1mg 3% DV.

Cheese and Sausage Stuffed Zucchini

Prep: 30 mins **Cook:** 40 mins **Total:** 1 hr 10 mins **Servings:** 5 **Yield:** 5 servings

Ingredients

- 12 ounces pork sausage
- 1 large zucchini
- 3 large eggs eggs, beaten
- 1 cup shredded Colby cheese
- 2 cups cottage cheese
- 1 ½ cups shredded Italian cheese blend
- ½ cup chopped onion
- 2 tablespoons Italian seasoning
- ½ teaspoon salt
- ½ teaspoon ground black pepper
- 1 pinch garlic salt
- ½ cup chopped tomatoes

Directions

Step 1

Preheat oven to 350 degrees F (175 degrees C). Butter a baking dish (size is dependent on the size of your zucchini).

Step 2

Place crumbled sausage in a large, deep skillet. Cook over medium high heat until evenly brown. Drain and set aside.

Step 3

Partially cook zucchini in the microwave on high for 5 minutes. Remove from the microwave and let cool for about 10 minutes. Meanwhile, in a medium bowl combine eggs, Colby cheese, cottage cheese, Italian blend cheese, onion, Italian seasoning, salt and pepper.

Step 4

Slice the zucchini in half lengthwise, remove the seeds and rinse. Place both halves in prepared baking dish and sprinkle with garlic salt. Layer the sausage, tomatoes and cheese mixture in each half.

Step 5

Bake in preheated oven for 40 minutes. Then broil for 5 minutes to brown the cheese.

Nutrition Facts

Per Serving:

649.4 calories; protein 37.6g 75% DV; carbohydrates 10.5g 3% DV; fat 51g 79% DV; cholesterol 218.9mg 73% DV; sodium 1630.2mg 65% DV.

Pumpkin Gingerbread

Prep: 15 mins Cook: 45 mins Total: 1 hr Servings: 24 Yield: 2 - 9x5 inch loaves

Ingredients

- 3 cups sugar
- 1 cup vegetable oil
- 4 large eggs eggs
- ⅔ cup water
- 1 (15 ounce) can pumpkin puree
- 2 teaspoons ground ginger
- 1 teaspoon ground allspice
- 1 teaspoon ground cinnamon
- 1 teaspoon ground cloves
- 3 ½ cups all-purpose flour
- 2 teaspoons baking soda
- 1 ½ teaspoons salt
- ½ teaspoon baking powder

Directions

Step 1

Preheat oven to 350 degrees F (175 degrees C). Lightly grease two 9x5 inch loaf pans.

Step 2

In a large mixing, combine sugar, oil and eggs; beat until smooth. Add water and beat until well blended. Stir in pumpkin, ginger, allspice cinnamon, and clove.

Step 3

In medium bowl, combine flour, soda, salt, and baking powder. Add dry ingredients to pumpkin mixture and blend just until all ingredients are mixed. Divide batter between prepared pans.

Step 4

Bake in preheated oven until toothpick comes out clean, about 1 hour.

Nutrition Facts

Per Serving:

262.6 calories; protein 3.2g 6% DV; carbohydrates 40.7g 13% DV; fat 10.2g 16% DV; cholesterol 31mg 10% DV; sodium 313.1mg 13% DV.

Dutch Apple Pie

Servings: 8 Yield: 1 - 9 inch pie

Ingredients

- 5 large Granny Smith apples - peeled, cored and sliced

- ½ cup white sugar
- 2 tablespoons all-purpose flour
- ½ teaspoon ground cinnamon
- 2 tablespoons lemon juice
- ½ cup white sugar
- ½ cup all-purpose flour
- ½ cup butter
- 1 recipe pastry for a 9 inch single crust pie

Directions

Step 1

Preheat oven to 425 degrees F (220 degrees C).

Step 2

Combine 1/2 cup sugar, 2 tablespoons flour, and cinnamon. Pour over apples in crust. Sprinkle lemon juice on top.

Step 3

Cut 1/2 cup sugar, 1/2 cup flour, and 1/2 cup butter or margarine together, and top pie with the mixture.

Step 4

Take two 15 inch pieces of parchment paper and enclose pie; fold edges up 3 times. Place on a baking sheet.

Step 5

Bake in preheated oven for 1 hour. Remove from oven, split parchment open and cool pie on wire rack. DO NOT open parchment covering while baking! Serve warm, or at room temperature.

Nutrition Facts

Per Serving:

407.3 calories; protein 2.9g 6% DV; carbohydrates 59.6g 19% DV; fat 19.1g 29% DV; cholesterol 30.5mg 10% DV; sodium 200.2mg 8% DV.

Bulk Venison Breakfast Sausage

Prep: 45 mins **Total:** 45 mins **Servings:** 64 **Yield:** 8 pounds

Ingredients

- 6 pounds ground venison
- 2 pounds ground pork
- ¼ cup sugar-based curing mixture (such as Morton Tender Quick)
- 1 tablespoon fresh-ground black pepper
- 1 tablespoon crushed red pepper flakes
- ¼ cup packed brown sugar

- 3 tablespoons dried sage

Directions

Step 1

In a very large bowl or plastic tub, sprinkle the venison and pork with the curing mixture, pepper, pepper flakes, sugar, and sage. Mix very well to evenly incorporate everything. When working with large quantitie of sausage, cook a small piece to make sure the seasoning is exactly how you like it.

Step 2

Divide into 1 pound portions and freeze.

Nutrition Facts

Per Serving:

92.6 calories; protein 12.2g 24% DV; carbohydrates 1g; fat 4.1g 6% DV; cholesterol 46.4mg 16% DV; sodium 472.1mg 19% DV.

Arugula-Fennel Salad

Prep: 15 mins **Total:** 15 mins **Servings:** 6 **Yield:** 6 servings

Ingredients

- ⅓ cup extra-virgin olive oil
- ½ teaspoon salt
- 1 teaspoon lemon zest
- ¼ cup fresh lemon juice
- 6 cups arugula
- 2 small fennel bulbs, cored and thinly sliced
- ½ cup toasted pine nuts
- 30 eaches grape tomatoes, halved
- ½ cup freshly grated Parmesan cheese

Directions

Step 1

Make the dressing by whisking the olive oil, salt, lemon zest, and lemon juice together in a small bowl; set aside. Place the arugula leaves into a large salad bowl. Sprinkle the fennel, pine nuts, grape tomatoes, and Parmesan cheese over top. Toss with the lemon dressing immediately before serving.

Nutrition Facts

Per Serving:

244.3 calories; protein 7.1g 14% DV; carbohydrates 10.7g 4% DV; fat 20.6g 32% DV; cholesterol 5.9mg 2% DV; sodium 332.6mg 13% DV.

Cheesy Meatloaf

Prep: 15 mins **Cook:** 1 hr **Total:** 1 hr 15 mins **Servings:** 8 **Yield:** 8 servings

Ingredients

- 1 pound ground beef
- 1 pound ground pork
- 1 (1 ounce) envelope dry onion soup mix
- 2 large eggs eggs, beaten
- 1 ½ cups dry bread crumbs
- ground black pepper to taste
- ¾ cup water
- 2 cups shredded mozzarella cheese, divided

Directions

Step 1

Preheat oven to 350 degrees F (175 degrees C).

Step 2

In a large bowl combine the beef, pork, soup mix, eggs, bread crumbs, pepper and water. Stir in 1/2 cup of the cheese. Mix well and spread half of mixture into a 9x5 inch loaf pan. Spread remaining 1 1/2 cups cheese over meat loaf mixture. Top with remaining half of meat loaf mixture.

Step 3

Bake in preheated oven for 60 minutes. Let cool 10 to 15 minutes before serving.

Nutrition Facts

Per Serving:

407.6 calories; protein 30.4g 61% DV; carbohydrates 17.6g 6% DV; fat 23.2g 36% DV; cholesterol 135.5mg 45% DV; sodium 701.9mg 28% DV.

Steak N Gravy

Prep: 30 mins **Cook:** 1 hr **Total:** 1 hr 30 mins **Servings:** 4 **Yield:** 4 servings

Ingredients

- 4 (4 ounce) venison steaks
- 1 cup all-purpose flour
- 2 tablespoons ground bay leaves
- 1 pinch salt and pepper
- 4 tablespoons olive oil, divided
- ½ onion, chopped

- 6 medium (blank)s fresh mushrooms, sliced
- 1 tablespoon minced garlic
- 1 (10.5 ounce) can beef gravy
- ¼ cup milk

Directions

Step 1

Cut all fat and gristle off the meat, and pound each steak out with a meat tenderizer until they are thin but not tearing. In a shallow bowl, combine flour, bay leaf, salt and pepper. Dredge steaks in the flour mixture until evenly coated.

Step 2

Heat 1 tablespoon olive oil in a large heavy skillet over medium heat. Saute onions until soft and translucent. Stir in mushrooms and garlic, and cook until tender. Remove from skillet and set aside. Heat remaining oil, and fry each steak for 2 minutes on each side, or until golden brown. Return onion mixture to skillet. Stir in gravy and milk. Reduce heat, cover, and simmer for 30 to 40 minutes. Stir occasionally to prevent sticking.

Nutrition Facts

Per Serving:

424.3 calories; protein 32.1g 64% DV; carbohydrates 32.2g 10% DV; fat 18g 28% DV; cholesterol 100.7mg 34% DV; sodium 498.1mg 20% DV.

Blushing Applesauce

Prep: 30 mins **Cook:** 25 mins **Total:** 55 mins **Servings:** 10 **Yield:** 10 servings

Ingredients

- 5 pounds Macintosh apples, quartered and cored
- ¾ cup sugar
- ¾ cup water
- ¼ cup lemon juice
- 1 teaspoon cinnamon
- ½ teaspoon nutmeg

Directions

Step 1

Place apples in a large pot with the sugar, water, and lemon juice. Bring to a boil, then reduce heat to medium-low and simmer uncovered, stirring occasionally, until the apples are very soft and lose their shape, about 25 minutes.

Step 2

Remove the apples from the heat and allow to cool slightly. Puree apples in a food processor or food mill. If using the food processor, strain the apples through a sieve to remove the pieces of apple skin.

Step 3

Stir in the cinnamon and nutmeg. Serve at room temperature or refrigerate and serve cold.

Nutrition Facts

Per Serving:

179 calories; protein 0.6g 1% DV; carbohydrates 47.1g 15% DV; fat 0.4g 1% DV; cholesterolmg; sodium 2.9mg.

Super Duper Easy Apple Cake

Prep: 15 mins **Cook:** 40 mins **Total:** 55 mins **Servings:** 14 **Yield:** 1 10-inch tube pan

Ingredients

- 1 (18.25 ounce) package yellow cake mix
- 1 tablespoon ground cinnamon
- 1 teaspoon vanilla extract
- 2 eaches Granny Smith apples - peeled, cored and finely diced

Directions

Step 1

Preheat oven to 350 degrees F (175 degrees C).

Step 2

Prepare cake mix according to package directions for a 10-inch tube pan. Stir in the cinnamon and vanilla extract, then fold in the chopped apples.

Step 3

Pour batter into prepared pan. Bake in the preheated oven until a toothpick inserted into the center of the cake comes out clean, about 40 minutes. Allow to cool.

Nutrition Facts

Per Serving:

170.3 calories; protein 1.7g 3% DV; carbohydrates 31.7g 10% DV; fat 4.3g 7% DV; cholesterol 0.7mg; sodium 242.9mg 10% DV.

Grilled Eggplant Moussaka

Prep: 50 mins **Cook:** 50 mins **Total:** 1 hr 40 mins **Servings:** 8 **Yield:** 1 9x13-inch pan

Ingredients

- 3 large eggplant, sliced into 1/4 inch rounds

- 3 large potatoes, thinly sliced
- 3 large zucchini, cut lengthwise into 1/4 inch slices
- ½ cup extra-virgin olive oil
- 5 tablespoons butter
- 7 tablespoons all-purpose flour
- 5 cups milk
- 1 pinch ground nutmeg
- 1 pinch salt to taste
- 1 egg yolk, beaten
- 1 tablespoon olive oil
- 1 ½ pounds ground beef
- 1 onion, chopped
- 1 teaspoon oregano
- 1 pinch salt and pepper to taste
- ½ cup chopped fresh parsley
- 5 medium whole (2-3/5" dia) (blank)s ripe tomatoes, chopped
- 1 cup crumbled feta cheese

Directions

Step 1

Preheat an outdoor grill for medium-high heat and lightly oil grate.

Step 2

Brush eggplant, potatoes, and zucchini lightly with extra-virgin olive oil. Grill vegetables until just tender and golden brown. Layer potatoes into the bottom of a 9x13 inch glass baking dish. Next layer in the eggplant, followed by the zucchini; set aside.

Step 3

Preheat oven to 375 degrees F (190 degrees C).

Step 4

Melt butter in a large saucepan over medium heat. Whisk in the flour, and cook until the flour smells slightly toasted, about 5 minutes. Whisk in milk, nutmeg, and salt. Bring to a bare simmer over medium-high heat, then reduce heat to medium-low and simmer 10 minutes. Place the egg yolk into a bowl, and quickly whisk in 1/4 cup of the thickened milk, a tablespoon at a time. Quickly stir the egg yolk mixture into the thickened milk until smooth, then set aside.

Step 5

Meanwhile, heat 1 tablespoon of olive oil in a large skillet over medium-high heat. Stir in the ground beef and onion, and cook until the beef is crumbly and no longer pink. Drain off any excess grease, then stir in the oregano, parsley, tomatoes, salt, and pepper. Turn heat to medium-low, cover, and simmer for 10 minutes, stirring occasionally.

Step 6

To assemble, spread the meat mixture over the vegetables, and sprinkle with the feta cheese. Pour the white sauce overtop, and smooth with a spatula.

Step 7

Bake moussaka in preheated oven until bubbly and golden brown, about 30 minutes.

Nutrition Facts

Per Serving:

721.8 calories; protein 30.9g 62% DV; carbohydrates 60.7g 20% DV; fat 41.6g 64% DV; cholesterol 125.3mg 42% DV; sodium 405.2mg 16% DV.

Apple Butter Pork Loin

Prep: 15 mins **Cook:** 3 hrs **Total:** 3 hrs 15 mins **Servings:** 6 **Yield:** 6 servings

Ingredients

- 2 (2 pound) boneless pork loin roast
- seasoning salt to taste
- 2 cups apple juice
- ½ cup apple butter
- ¼ cup brown sugar
- 2 tablespoons water
- ¼ teaspoon ground cinnamon
- ¼ teaspoon ground cloves

Directions

Step 1

Preheat the oven to 350 degrees F (175 degrees C).

Step 2

Season the pork loins with seasoning salt, and place them in a 9x13 inch baking dish or small roasting pan. Pour apple juice over the pork, and cover the dish with a lid or aluminum foil.

Step 3

Bake for 1 hour in the preheated oven. While the pork is roasting, mix together the apple butter, brown sugar, water, cinnamon, and cloves. Remove pork roasts from the oven, and spread with apple butter mixture.

Step 4

Cover, and return to the oven for 2 hours, or until fork-tender.

Nutrition Facts

Per Serving:

606.5 calories; protein 64.9g 130% DV; carbohydrates 25.7g 8% DV; fat 25.4g 39% DV; cholesterol 194.1mg 65% DV; sodium 150.6mg 6% DV.

Best Zucchini Casserole

Prep: 30 mins **Cook:** 45 mins **Total:** 1 hr 15 mins **Servings:** 8 **Yield:** 8 servings

Ingredients

- 8 cups diced zucchini
- 1 red bell pepper, chopped
- 1 cup cornflakes cereal
- 1 cup shredded Cheddar cheese
- ½ cup olive oil
- 1 teaspoon dried basil
- 2 large eggs eggs, beaten
- salt and pepper to taste

Directions

Step 1

Preheat oven to 350 degrees F (175 degrees C). Lightly oil a 9x13 inch baking dish.

Step 2

In a large bowl, combine zucchini, bell pepper, cornflakes, cheese, oil, basil, and eggs. Season with salt and pepper to taste. Spread evenly into prepared baking dish.

Step 3

Bake in the preheated oven for 45 minutes, or until top is golden brown.

Nutrition Facts

Per Serving:

231.7 calories; protein 7g 14% DV; carbohydrates 8.5g 3% DV; fat 19.7g 30% DV; cholesterol 61.3mg 20% DV; sodium 143.8mg 6% DV.

Dutch Apple Cake

Servings: 15 **Yield:** 7 x 11 inch cake

Ingredients

- ½ cup shortening
- 1 cup white sugar
- 1 egg

- 1 ½ teaspoons vanilla extract
- 1 ½ cups all-purpose flour
- 1 tablespoon baking powder
- ½ teaspoon salt
- ¾ cup milk
- 2 medium (2-3/4" dia) (approx 3 per lb)s apples - peeled, cored and cut into eighths
- ¼ cup white sugar
- 1 teaspoon ground cinnamon

Directions

Step 1

Sift flour with baking powder and salt.

Step 2

In a large bowl, cream shortening and 1 cup sugar until light. Beat in egg and vanilla until fluffy. Add sifted ingredients to the creamed mixture alternately with milk, beginning and ending with the sifted ingredients. Spread the batter into a greased 7 x 11 inch baking pan.

Step 3

Place apple pieces in rows on the batter with the sharp edges pressed in slightly. Sprinkle 1/4 cup sugar and cinnamon on top.

Step 4

Bake at 350 degrees F (175 degrees C) for about 50 to 60 minutes, or until the apples are tender and the cake tests done.

Nutrition Facts

Per Serving:

193 calories; protein 2.2g 4% DV; carbohydrates 29.8g 10% DV; fat 7.6g 12% DV; cholesterol 13.4mg 5% DV; sodium 185.2mg 7% DV.

Chicken Savoy

Prep: 10 mins **Cook:** 1 hr **Total:** 1 hr 10 mins **Servings:** 4 **Yield:** 4 servings

Ingredients

- 1 (2 to 3 pound) whole chicken, cut into pieces
- ⅛ cup extra virgin olive oil
- 1 cup chicken stock
- 1 clove garlic, crushed
- 1 teaspoon dried oregano
- salt and pepper to taste

- ¼ cup grated Romano cheese
- 3 tablespoons balsamic vinegar

Directions

Step 1

Preheat oven to 450 degrees F (230 degrees C).

Step 2

Place chicken pieces in a 9x13 inch baking dish. Pour oil and stock over chicken and sprinkle with garlic. Season with oregano, salt and pepper and top with cheese.

Step 3

Bake in the preheated oven for about 45 to 60 minutes, or until chicken is cooked through and no longer pink inside.

Step 4

Pour vinegar over chicken and serve.

Cook's Note:

You can use red wine vinegar in place of the balsamic.

Nutrition Facts

Per Serving:

477.2 calories; protein 45.4g 91% DV; carbohydrates 2.9g 1% DV; fat 30.4g 47% DV; cholesterol 178.6mg 60% DV; sodium 389.7mg 16% DV.

Awesome Eggplant Rollatine

Prep: 20 mins **Cook:** 45 mins **Total:** 1 hr 5 mins **Servings:** 4 **Yield:** 4 servings

Ingredients

- 4 large eggs eggs, lightly beaten
- 2 tablespoons garlic powder, divided
- 2 cups grated Parmesan cheese, divided
- 1 tablespoon Italian seasoning
- salt and pepper to taste
- 1 cup all-purpose flour
- 1 cup vegetable oil for frying
- 2 eggplant, peeled (yield from 1.25 lb)s large eggplant, peeled and sliced
- 1 (15 ounce) container ricotta cheese
- 1 cup shredded mozzarella cheese, divided
- 1 tablespoon dried parsley
- 1 (10 ounce) package frozen chopped spinach, thawed and drained

- 1 (28 ounce) jar tomato pasta sauce, divided

Directions

Step 1

Preheat oven to 350 degrees F (175 degrees C).

Step 2

In a shallow mixing bowl combine 3 eggs, 1 tablespoon garlic powder, 1 cup Parmesan cheese, Italian seasoning, salt and pepper. In a separate, shallow dish or plate, pour the flour.

Step 3

Heat oil in a large, deep skillet. Dredge eggplant slices in flour, then in egg mixture and fry slices 2 or 3 at a time in hot oil. Place fried slices on a paper towel lined plate to drain.

Step 4

In a large bowl combine ricotta, 1/2 cup mozzarella, remaining 1 cup Parmesan, remaining 1 tablespoon garlic powder, 1 egg, parsley and spinach; mix well.

Step 5

Spread about 1/3 of the pasta sauce in the bottom of a 9x13 inch baking dish. Place about 2 tablespoons of spinach mixture in the center of each eggplant slice and roll securely; place in prepared pan. Pour remaining pasta sauce over eggplant rolls and top with remaining 1/2 cup mozzarella cheese.

Step 6

Bake in preheated oven for 30 minutes.

Nutrition Facts

Per Serving:

894.4 calories; protein 53.3g 107% DV; carbohydrates 79.6g 26% DV; fat 41.6g 64% DV; cholesterol 276.2mg 92% DV; sodium 1872mg 75% DV.

Pumpkin Dessert

Prep: 10 mins **Cook:** 50 mins **Total:** 1 hr **Servings:** 18 **Yield:** 1 9x13 inch baking dish

Ingredients

- 1 (18.25 ounce) package yellow cake mix
- ⅓ cup butter, melted
- 1 egg
- 1 (29 ounce) can pumpkin
- ½ cup brown sugar
- .66 cup milk
- 3 large eggs eggs
- 2 tablespoons pumpkin pie spice

- ¼ cup butter, chilled
- ½ cup white sugar
- ¾ cup chopped walnuts

Directions

Step 1

Preheat oven to 350 degrees F (175 degrees C) and lightly grease a 9x13 inch baking dish.

Step 2

Set aside 1 cup of cake mix. Combine remaining cake mix with melted butter and 1 egg and mix until well blended; spread mixture in the bottom of the prepared baking dish.

Step 3

In a large bowl combine pumpkin, brown sugar, milk, 3 eggs and pumpkin pie spice; mix well and pour this mixture over cake mix mixture in baking dish.

Step 4

In a small bowl with a pastry blender, or in a food processor, combine chilled butter and white sugar with reserved cake mix until mixture resembles coarse crumbs. Sprinkle over pumpkin mixture. Sprinkle chopped walnuts over all.

Step 5

Bake 45 to 50 minutes, until top is golden.

Nutrition Facts

Per Serving:

291.8 calories; protein 4.6g 9% DV; carbohydrates 39.1g 13% DV; fat 14.1g 22% DV; cholesterol 58.3mg 19% DV; sodium 254.1mg 10% DV.

Pumpkin Cookies with Cream Cheese Frosting (The World's Best!)

Prep: 30 mins **Cook:** 10 mins **Additional:** 30 mins **Total:** 1 hr 10 mins **Servings:** 36 **Yield:** 3 dozen cookies

Ingredients

- 2 cups all-purpose flour
- 1 teaspoon baking powder
- 1 teaspoon ground cinnamon
- ½ teaspoon baking soda
- ½ teaspoon ground nutmeg
- ½ teaspoon ground ginger

- 1 cup butter
- ¾ cup white sugar
- ¾ cup brown sugar
- 2 teaspoons vanilla extract
- 1 egg
- 1 (15 ounce) can pumpkin puree
- 1 (3 ounce) package cream cheese, softened
- ¼ cup butter, softened
- 1 teaspoon vanilla extract
- 2 cups confectioners' sugar

Directions

Step 1

Preheat oven to 350 degrees F (175 degrees C). Lightly grease baking sheets.

Step 2

Whisk flour, baking powder, cinnamon, baking soda, nutmeg, and ginger together in a bowl. Beat 1 cup butter, white sugar, brown sugar, 2 teaspoons vanilla extract, and egg with an electric mixer in a separate large bowl, beating until mixture is smooth. Beat in pumpkin puree. Gradually stir dry ingredients into pumpkin mixture. Batter will be moist.

Step 3

Spoon batter by teaspoonfuls about 2 inches apart onto prepared baking sheets.

Step 4

Bake in the preheated oven until cookies are lightly browned, 10 to 12 minutes. Let cookies cool for about 5 minutes on sheets before removing to finish cooling on waxed paper.

Step 5

Beat cream cheese, 1/4 cup butter, and 1 teaspoon vanilla extract in a bowl with an electric mixer until soft and creamy. Beat in confectioners' sugar, about 1/2 cup at a time, until frosting is smooth and spreadable. Frost cooled cookies with cream cheese frosting.

Nutrition Facts

Per Serving:

152.3 calories; protein 1.3g 3% DV; carbohydrates 20.6g 7% DV; fat 7.5g 12% DV; cholesterol 24.7mg 8% DV; sodium 115mg 5% DV.

Quick Brussels and Bacon

Prep: 15 mins **Cook:** 15 mins **Total:** 30 mins **Servings:** 6 **Yield:** 6 servings

Ingredients

- 6 slices bacon
- ½ tablespoon olive oil
- 3 eaches shallots, chopped
- 1 (16 ounce) package frozen Brussels sprouts, thawed and halved

Directions

Step 1

Cook the bacon in a large skillet over medium-high heat until crisp; drain on paper towels and crumble.

Step 2

Heat the olive oil in a large skillet over medium-high heat. Cook and stir the onion in the oil until soft; stir in the bacon and cook until bacon is heated through. Add the Brussels sprouts; cook and stir until the sprout are browned, 7 to 10 minutes.

Nutrition Facts

Per Serving:

188.7 calories; protein 6.4g 13% DV; carbohydrates 11.2g 4% DV; fat 14g 22% DV; cholesterol 19mg 6% DV; sodium 255.2mg 10% DV.

Banana Cranberry Bread

Prep: 15 mins **Cook:** 1 hr **Additional:** 15 mins **Total:** 1 hr 30 mins **Servings:** 24 **Yield:** 2 - 9x5 inch loave

Ingredients

- 2 ½ cups white sugar
- 1 cup shortening
- 3 large eggs eggs
- 3 medium (7" to 7-7/8" long)s mashed bananas
- 1 cup cranberry sauce
- ½ cup milk
- 1 teaspoon vanilla extract
- 4 cups all-purpose flour
- 1 ½ teaspoons baking soda
- 1 ½ teaspoons baking powder
- 1 teaspoon ground cinnamon
- ½ teaspoon ground nutmeg
- ½ cup chopped walnuts

Directions

Step 1

Preheat oven to 350 degrees F (175 degrees C). Lightly grease two 9x5 inch loaf pans.

Step 2

In a large bowl, cream together the sugar and shortening until light and fluffy. Beat in eggs, and mix in bananas, cranberry sauce, milk, and vanilla. In a separate bowl, mix together flour, baking soda, baking powder, cinnamon, and nutmeg. Gradually blend flour mixture into the banana mixture. Fold in walnuts. Pour into the prepared loaf pans.

Step 3

Bake for 50 to 60 minutes in the preheated oven, or until a toothpick inserted in the center comes out clean. Cool in pan for 10 minutes, then turn out onto a wire rack, and cool completely.

Nutrition Facts

Per Serving:

291.5 calories; protein 3.7g 7% DV; carbohydrates 45.4g 15% DV; fat 11.2g 17% DV; cholesterol 23.7mg 8% DV; sodium 116mg 5% DV.

Squash and Zucchini Casserole

Prep: 20 mins **Cook:** 30 mins **Total:** 50 mins **Servings:** 5 **Yield:** 4 servings

Ingredients

- 2 medium yellow squash
- 2 large zucchini
- 1 Vidalia onions, thinly sliced
- 2 large tomatoes, sliced
- 2 cups grated Romano cheese
- ½ cup butter, divided
- salt and pepper to taste

Directions

Step 1

Preheat oven to 375 degrees F (190 degrees C).

Step 2

Cut the zucchini and squash into long, thin layers. Lightly grease a 7x11-inch baking dish and layer the squash, zucchini, onion and tomatoes into the baking dish. Sprinkle with cheese and add pats of butter between each layer of vegetables, and season each layer with salt and ground black pepper to taste.

Step 3

Continue this layering process until all the vegetables are used up and top this off with the remaining butter and cheese.

Step 4

Cover and bake at 375 degrees F (190 degrees C) for 20 to 30 minutes, or until vegetables are to desired tenderness and cheese is melted and bubbly.

Sweet Potato Pie II

Prep: 20 mins **Cook:** 40 mins **Total:** 1 hr **Servings:** 8 **Yield:** 1 - 9 inch pie

Ingredients

- 2 cups mashed sweet potatoes
- ¼ pound butter, softened
- 2 large eggs eggs, separated
- 1 cup packed brown sugar
- ¼ teaspoon salt
- ½ teaspoon ground ginger
- ½ teaspoon ground cinnamon
- ½ teaspoon ground nutmeg
- ½ cup evaporated milk
- ¼ cup white sugar
- 1 (9 inch) unbaked pie crust

Directions

Step 1

Preheat oven to 400 degrees F (200 degrees C).

Step 2

In a mixing bowl, combine the sweet potatoes, butter, egg yolks, brown sugar, salt, ginger, cinnamon, nutmeg and evaporated milk. Mix together well.

Step 3

Beat egg whites until stiff peaks form; add 1/4 cup sugar and fold into sweet potato mixture.

Step 4

Pour into pie shell and bake at 400 degrees F (200 degrees C) for 10 minutes. Reduce heat and bake at 350 degrees F (175 degrees C) for 30 minutes or until firm.

Apple Breakfast Bread

Prep: 15 mins **Cook:** 1 hr **Additional:** 15 mins **Total:** 1 hr 30 mins **Servings:** 10 **Yield:** 10 servings

Ingredients

- ½ cup butter
- 1 cup sugar
- 2 large eggs eggs
- 2 cups all-purpose flour
- 1 teaspoon baking soda
- ½ teaspoon salt
- 1 teaspoon ground cinnamon
- ½ teaspoon ground cloves
- 2 medium (2-3/4" dia) (approx 3 per lb)s apples - peeled, cored and chopped

Directions

Step 1

Preheat oven to 350 degrees F (175 degrees C). Lightly grease an 8x4 inch loaf pan.

Step 2

In a bowl, mix the butter and sugar until smooth and creamy. Beat in the eggs.

Step 3

In a separate bowl, sift together the flour, baking soda, salt, cinnamon, and cloves. Mix into the butter mixture until moistened. Fold in the apples. Transfer to the prepared loaf pan.

Step 4

Bake 1 hour in the preheated oven, until a toothpick inserted in the center comes out clean. Cool in the pan for 15 minutes before removing to a wire rack to cool completely.

Nutrition Facts

Per Serving:

279.3 calories; protein 4g 8% DV; carbohydrates 43.2g 14% DV; fat 10.5g 16% DV; cholesterol 61.6mg 21% DV; sodium 322.6mg 13% DV.

Easy Swedish Apple Pie

Prep: 20 mins **Cook:** 45 mins **Total:** 1 hr 5 mins **Servings:** 8 **Yield:** 1 - 9 inch pie

Ingredients

- 1 ½ pounds Granny Smith apples - peeled, cored and sliced
- 1 tablespoon sugar
- 1 cup sugar

- 1 cup flour
- 1 teaspoon cinnamon
- ¾ cup melted butter
- 1 egg

Directions

Step 1

Preheat oven to 350 degrees F (175 degrees C).

Step 2

Toss apples with 1 tablespoon of sugar, and pour them into a pie plate. Thoroughly mix together 1 cup of sugar with the flour, cinnamon, butter, and egg. Spread this evenly over the top of the pie.

Step 3

Bake in preheated oven until the apples have cooked and the topping is golden brown, about 40 to 45 minutes.

Nutrition Facts

Per Serving:

359.4 calories; protein 2.8g 6% DV; carbohydrates 49.3g 16% DV; fat 18g 28% DV; cholesterol 69mg 23% DV; sodium 132.5mg 5% DV.

Zucchini with Chickpea and Mushroom Stuffing

Prep: 30 mins **Cook:** 30 mins **Total:** 1 hr **Servings:** 8 **Yield:** 8 servings

Ingredients

- 4 medium (blank)s zucchini, halved
- 1 tablespoon olive oil
- 1 onion, chopped
- 2 cloves garlic, crushed
- ½ (8 ounce) package button mushrooms, sliced
- 1 teaspoon ground coriander
- 1 ½ teaspoons ground cumin, or to taste
- 1 (15.5 ounce) can chickpeas, rinsed and drained
- ½ lemon, juiced
- 2 tablespoons chopped fresh parsley
- sea salt to taste
- ground black pepper to taste

Directions

Step 1

Preheat oven to 350 degrees F (175 degrees C). Grease a shallow baking dish.

Step 2

Scoop out the flesh of the zucchini; chop the flesh and set aside. Place the shells in the prepared dish.

Step 3

Heat oil in a large skillet over medium heat. Saute onions for 5 minutes, then add garlic and saute 2 minutes more. Stir in chopped zucchini and mushrooms; saute 5 minutes. Stir in coriander, cumin, chickpeas, lemon juice, parsley, salt and pepper. Spoon mixture into zucchini shells.

Step 4

Bake in preheated oven for 30 to 40 minutes, or until zucchini are tender.

Nutrition Facts
Per Serving:
107.4 calories; protein 4.5g 9% DV; carbohydrates 18.4g 6% DV; fat 2.7g 4% DV; cholesterolmg; sodium 170mg 7% DV.

Mexican Zucchini Cheese Soup

Prep: 20 mins **Cook:** 25 mins **Total:** 45 mins **Servings:** 6 **Yield:** 6 Servings

Ingredients

- 1 tablespoon olive oil
- 1 cup chopped onion
- 2 cloves garlic, minced
- ½ teaspoon dried oregano
- 2 (14.5 ounce) cans chicken broth
- 1 (14.5 ounce) can Mexican-style stewed tomatoes
- 2 medium zucchini, halved lengthwise and cut in 1/4 inch slices
- 2 medium (blank)s medium yellow squash, halved lengthwise and cut in 1/4 inch slices
- 1 (8.75 ounce) can whole kernel corn, drained
- 1 (4.5 ounce) can diced green chile peppers
- 12 ounces processed cheese food, cubed
- ½ teaspoon freshly ground black pepper
- ¼ cup chopped fresh cilantro

Directions
Step 1

Heat the olive oil in a large pot, and saute the onion and garlic until tender. Season with oregano.

Step 2

Mix in the chicken broth and tomatoes. Bring to a boil. Mix in the zucchini, yellow squash, corn, and chile peppers. Reduce heat to low, and simmer 10 minutes, or until the squash is tender.

Step 3

Mix the cubed processed cheese into the soup. Continue to cook and stir until cheese is melted. Season with pepper. Mix in the cilantro just before serving.

Nutrition Facts

Per Serving:

306.7 calories; protein 14.7g 29% DV; carbohydrates 26.2g 9% DV; fat 17.5g 27% DV; cholesterol 47.8mg 16% DV; sodium 1829mg 73% DV.